# Building the

## A Rugby Lea

## Maurice Oldroyd

## London League Publications Ltd

## Building the family game
## A Rugby League Memoir

A CIP catalogue record for this book is available from the British Library.

First published in Great Britain in August 2014 by London League Publications Ltd, PO Box 65784, London NW2 9NS

ISBN: 978-1909885-05-9

Cover design by Stephen McCarthy Graphic Design, 46, Clarence Road, London N15 5BB

Editing and layout by Peter Lush

Printed and bound in Great Britain by Charlesworth Press, Wakefield

## This book is dedicated to
## the memory of my wife, Mary.

# Foreword

Maurice and I have never fallen out. "That's good, but what has it to do with anything?" folk reasonably ask.

Well, the fact is that throughout the long years when we headed up our respective governing bodies, BARLA and the RFL, they were all too often at war despite the combined efforts of us both to avert such damaging situations, though there were numerous occasions when we did succeed, quietly working together behind the scenes. Thus it was that during these years we built a deep friendship and mutual respect which endures to this day.

One of the best ways to get to know someone is to travel the world in their company. Maurice and I were regular delegates to Rugby League International Board meetings abroad. I well recall, on a free day in Papua New Guinea, the then RFL chairman, Bob Ashby, and I took Maurice, rather against his better judgement, on a visit to a somewhat hairy crocodile farm. Later Bob lamented that "It was a pity the crocs weren't biting that day". I asked: What did he have in mind? He replied: "Well, there were only three of us and I wasn't referring to thee or me." Characteristically, Maurice still falls about laughing whenever we recall this incident. He is nothing if not very thick-skinned, extremely resilient and utterly determined – essential qualities in anyone occupying influential positions in our great game.

Maurice has dedicated a huge amount of his life to the game – and not only as a prominent administrator. He was a typical nuggety and combative scrum-half, a Grade 1 touch-judge and (not many people know this!) for short time a talent scout for Leeds RLFC, long before the era of the Rhino.

All of us who are privileged to serve the game in any capacity could not succeed, or even survive, without the wholehearted support of our families. Maurice found such wonderful support and encouragement from his late wife, Mary, whose sudden and untimely death shook to the core all of us privileged to know and love her. I know Maurice still misses her terribly, but derives great solace from son Adam and his delightful grandchildren, to whom he is very close.

I was delighted the Rugby League International Federation honoured Maurice with their prestigious Spirit of Rugby League award in 2013. I had previously been so honoured and I feel, somehow, this has drawn us even closer in our advancing years. I was, therefore, proud and touched to be invited to write this foreword to a volume which all who love rugby league will find most interesting and instructive.

## David Oxley CBE

David Oxley was chief executive of the Rugby Football League from 1975 to 1992, and is widely respected throughout the sport. This was reflected in his appointment to the honorary position of RFL president for one year in July 2013.

# A message from BARLA

Maurice Oldroyd, to coin a phrase Uncle Albert of *Only Fools and Horses* 'has served rugby league for over 70 years from man and boy', celebrated his 78th birthday last year. Maurice is one of the 'old school' of BARLA. He is currently the patron of the organisation and, as he has done from its formation in 1973, has always promoted BARLA and the positives of it all over the world where rugby league is played.

One thing that Maurice believes in with a passion is that once an agreement is made, all parties within that agreement 'Should stick to the rules'. These were watchwords of a great friend of his, Lord Lofthouse of Pontefract, who Maurice knew simply as 'Geoff', who sadly passed two years ago. These days when that doesn't go to plan, the watchword from other parties is 'We've moved on, we've drawn the line over it'.

If there is one thing that is set in stone in my head whenever I meet and speak to Maurice at board meetings or social functions relating to BARLA it is that 'BARLA and the RFL shall remain as separate organisations and for the avoidance of doubt the RFL shall not have the power either to amend the constitution of BARLA or to dissolve BARLA'.

In fact, and not to accelerate his passing, enshrined on his future headstone should be the words:
'For the avoidance of doubt BARLA and the RFL are two separate Bodies'. He has been involved in the game as a player, coach, referee and administrator as well as a fan of his beloved Huddersfield Giants.

Following all the hard, untold hours of work done by the late Tom Keaveney MBE and Jack Clayton, Maurice, who was then a referee, on 4 March 1973, attended the District Leagues meeting at Greenside Working Mens Club, Huddersfield. That day BARLA was formed. They broke away from the RFL because the amateurs did not have any say or vote in their own destiny and their sport was seriously declining. How ironic that 78 years earlier, in the same town the RFL, then known as the 'Northern Union' broke away from the RFU. On the night BARLA broke away with a £25 bank balance collected from the attendees.

Maurice is a proud man, even more so wearing his BARLA badged up blazer and the tie of all nations he was presented with at the 2004 Victory Cup in Moscow.

His proudest of many proud moments was in 1990 with the Royal Seal of approval for BARLA's community and voluntary youth work when Her Majesty The Queen opened BARLA's new Headquarters at West Yorkshire House in Huddersfield.

It is an honour to know you and long may you preach the name of BARLA.

**Steve Manning**
**BARLA vice chair**

### Publisher's note:
The obituary of Mary Oldroyd was first published in *Our Game*, issue 5, spring 2002.
The letter from the Australian Schoolboys RL is published with their permission.
The BARLA booklet published for their opening is reproduced with their permission.

# Introduction

I have always thought there was something Churchillian about Maurice Oldroyd, but have never been able to make up my mind whether he reminds me of Britain's revered war leader or of that dog off the telly. A bit of both, probably. There is certainly something of the bulldog about Maurice, not that he is irascible in nature, as I have met few more good-natured or generous men in my life. However, like the bulldog, he is incredibly tenacious, especially when it when it comes to holding on to an idea or a principle. Such a characteristic is usually viewed as praiseworthy, but politically may sometimes prove a handicap. The politics of amateur rugby league have undoubtedly left their mark on Maurice and *vice versa*.

The first time I met Maurice was at the George Hotel in Huddersfield, the birthplace of rugby league in 1895. The occasion was the 1993 launch of Yorkshire Arts Circus's celebrated book *When Push Comes to Shove*, edited by Ian Clayton. I think it was Ian who introduced me to Maurice after the proceedings drew to a close. I distinctly remember that we had an animated discussion about Maurice Lindsay and the way things were going in rugby league. Needless to say, neither of us was happy.

Although that was the start of a friendship, which has now lasted for more than two decades, Maurice had been a familiar figure to me – and anyone with more than a passing interest in rugby league – since 1973. For 20 years already his face had been beaming out of the pages of the rugby league press and his words had been heard on radio and television, as he remorselessly proclaimed the merits of amateur rugby league and its ruling body, the British Amateur Rugby League Association. BARLA was, he never tired of telling the world, "the sporting success story of the 70s, the 80s, the 90s, the century," depending on when he happened to be interviewed. For a long time he was right – BARLA was beyond a doubt a wonderful success. In its own way the creation of BARLA in 1973 was as huge an event as the creation of the Northern Union in 1895. To most rugby league people, Maurice and BARLA became almost synonymous. He was a founding father of the association, along with fellow stalwarts Tom Keavney, its first secretary, and Jack Clayton, its first chairman. Maurice filled the posts of assistant secretary, treasurer and PRO before becoming BARLA's first paid official with the title of national administrator. He subsequently transmogrified into BARLA's chief executive and when he retired at 65 he followed up by being elected as BARLA chairman and ultimately as patron, a position he still holds.

BARLA has been going for 41 years and Maurice has been at its heart for all that time, over half his life. No man has contributed more to amateur rugby league. Unlike his fellow BARLA *alumni*, Tom Keavney MBE, Jackie Reid MBE, Harold Swift MBE, Bob Beal OBE and Jack Clayton (Queen's Silver Jubilee Medal), Maurice has never been publicly honoured. He has, however, been serially recognised by the game itself, which may be more gratifying for him in the greater scheme of things. In 1990 he won the Rugby League Writers' Merit Award and in 1999 was awarded the All-Party Parliamentary Rugby League Merit Award. BARLA made him a Life Member in 2005 and he was admitted to the Rugby League Roll of Honour in the same year. Just last year (2013) the Rugby League International Federation conferred its Spirit of Rugby League Award on Maurice "in recognition of his commitment to international development over more than four decades."

Maurice and I lived in close proximity until 2008, when I moved to Wales. Maurice still lives in Greetland, between Halifax and Huddersfield, while I lived over the hill from him in Ripponden. In the few miles between our two houses lie the grounds of Greetland All-Rounders ARLC and Elland ARLC, while Siddal ARLC, one of the top amateur clubs in the country, is no more than a couple of miles from Maurice's house. It is totally appropriate that Maurice should reside in such a hotbed of amateur rugby league. He could not get away from the game if he wanted to.

Sometimes I felt that I could not get away from Maurice. He always seemed to be everywhere I went if it concerned rugby – amateur matches, professional matches, book launches, museum exhibitions. Life became much more complicated and interesting for me in 2001. That was when Maurice retired from his paid job at BARLA, not that he has ever really stopped working for BARLA. His big problem was that retirement meant he had no secretarial resources at his disposal and, what is more, he is a technophobe – totally, almost frighteningly, clueless. To be fair, I am not much better. However, Maurice realised I could type, could string a few words together and had a computer and a printer. For several years prior to his retirement he became a regular visitor to our house and particularly my office. To all intents and purposes I had become his secretary. I did not mind too much. I typed his letters to the great, the good and the downright horrible, proof-read his reports and submissions to amateur and professional colleagues, politicians, administrators and newspaper editors. I got to see how he worked – damned hard – and how he thought – carefully and strategically. I also got to realise just how labyrinthine the politics of amateur rugby league could be.

To have survived and thrived in that environment was a testimony to his well-honed political instincts, his ability to absorb punishment and his determination to do his best for the sport he loved, lived and breathed. I realised that being Churchillian was not enough and that a touch of Machiavellian, even from Maurice, was required to prosper in the murky world of rugby league politics.

Anyway, Maurice spent countless hours in Ripponden and was sometimes reprimanded by Mary for outstaying his welcome. People had better things to do than put up with him for hour after hour, she would say. My wife Myfanwy and I did not begrudge him the time. He is after all one of the friendliest of men, extremely sociable and amusing and, most importantly, genuinely interested in people and their welfare. Mind you, even if he did not exactly eat us out of house and home, he was always ready for Welsh cakes and coffee. Maurice will eat almost anything that appears before him and has a voraciously sweet tooth. Even so, he is very proud of having all his own teeth and says he has never had so much as a filling.

There was, however, definitely something wrong with him one Saturday night in my office. It was the autumn of 2000; not long before he was due to retire. I was seated at the keyboard waiting for Maurice to find the right word to finish off his sentence – these things could take a long time when Maurice was after his *juste mot*. He was standing just behind me to the right of the desk, a big, heavy piece of furniture. The next thing I knew, there was a thud and Maurice was on his knees with his forehead having smacked into the corner of the desk. I don't know who was most shocked – Maurice, the desk or me. Myfanwy and I looked after him for several hours, followed him home to make sure that he was all right and that Mary was aware of what had happened to him. The upshot was that Maurice was fitted with a pacemaker, which has subsequently worn out, and he is onto another.

If anyone thought that this would have slowed him down, they were to be sadly mistaken. Even now, 14 years later, in his late 70s and having recently had a new hip, Maurice remains a busy man. Function follows function, match follows match, meeting follows meeting. His itinerary beggars belief. According to my computer, this book was commenced on 16 February, 2008 at 17.10:32 precisely. That is not really true. That was just the time that I started typing the first chapter. There had been a lot of preparation, maybe two years, before we got to that stage. Because of his whirlwind way of operating Maurice was pretty hard to pin down. There was always something else to do. Basically, after three and a half chapters I gave up on it and told him to call me when his schedule calmed down. In the meantime I decamped to live in Wales, although we always kept in touch with Maurice promising to find time to finish the book. He never could find time, so I had to make arrangements myself. This necessitated actually living with him in Greetland for two separate weeks, the second of which was thankfully less frenetic because he had just had that hip operation, was practically a prisoner in his own house and could not even put his socks on. I shouldn't laugh.

It is fair to say that I greatly admire Maurice, but I certainly do not agree with him on all matters rugby league. I am therefore at pains to point out that, although I have typed the manuscript and sorted out the chronology of Maurice's tale, the text is as near to what he actually told me as I could manage. Left to my own devices, I would have been much more critical of some of the characters who have at various times attacked, undermined and criticised him, but that is not Maurice's way. Although perceived by some of his detractors as stubborn and reactionary, Maurice is slow to anger and remarkably forgiving of those who trespass against him. There have certainly been dirty tricks against him by people of whom better would be expected. Maurice would have every reason to hold grudges, but it is not in his nature. He knows that in politics, even sporting politics, there will be times of difficulty and adversaries will say and do what they think necessary to get their way. When issues have been settled, in his favour or not, personal animosity is cast aside and Maurice simply gets on with doing his best for BARLA.

Maurice has certainly had plenty of adversaries in his 40 odd years of service to amateur rugby league. He has struggled against the Rugby Football League, the Rugby Football Union, the National Conference League and various other elements in the amateur game. With friends like these, who needs enemies? The RFL was BARLA's biggest obstacle in its infancy and its secretary and main power broker, Bill Fallowfield, was initially no lover of Maurice Oldroyd, although they soon became reconciled. Maurice Bamford recalled that he and the Australian Garth Budge were involved in a coaching session with Fallowfield as BARLA were struggling to gain recognition. Bill asked Maurice Bamford about "Oldroyd and some of his chums. What's he like?" Bamford assured him that Oldroyd was a good man and that it would be sensible for the Rugby Football League to cooperate with the BARLA boys. Bill was not best pleased and told Bamford, "If I let that happen it would be the tail wagging the dog."

BARLA's detractors at times seemed to be more hostile to the amateur game than to the old enemy rugby union. At one point Bob Ashby, the RFL chairman, vowed to crush BARLA, while in later years Richard Lewis, the RFL executive chairman, famously declared that BARLA was "not fit for purpose". Maurice told me that in the years around the creation of Super League he sometimes felt battered from pillar to post, as he was having to contend with Maurice Lindsay, the most powerful man in rugby league, Rodney Walker, the most powerful man in British sport and Rupert Murdoch, one of the most powerful men in the world.

Down the years Maurice survived his tribulations in the game and invariably came up smiling. His characteristic doggedness, persistence, attention to detail and devotion to BARLA's preservation, combined with a certain charm and charisma, was usually enough to ward off internal and external challenges. It was very hard to dislike Maurice, whose *forte* was unquestionably his passion for networking. Maurice seems to know just about everybody. He was better at public relations than the professional PROs and never passed up an opportunity to put BARLA in the media spotlight. Maurice is not a vain man, but he has always known the value of a photo opportunity. He was probably an expert in exploiting that practice before the term had been coined. He also knew the importance of engaging with politicians, local and national, and with sports administrators, national and international. He made it his business to send relevant important people masses of cuttings about BARLA and rugby league in general – "to keep them in touch". Just as crucially, it also kept him in touch with them.

Maurice considered it essential to foster good relationships with the All-Party Parliamentary Rugby League Group and was particularly pleased when Geoffrey Lofthouse, the Deputy Speaker of the House of Commons, agreed to become BARLA president. For a man with such a depth of political experience his entry into rugby league politics was a bit of a shock. In 1999 Lord Lofthouse wrote in his autobiography *From Coalsack to Woolsack* "After becoming President I found it surprising, in view of BARLA's success, that all was not sweetness and light; the amateurs and professionals were at each other's throats". He also wrote, "Maurice Oldroyd, the chief executive of BARLA for 22 years, has worked relentlessly in his own special manner. The whole of the rugby league world, both professional and amateur, should be indebted to him."

Lord Lofthouse was far from the only luminary who held Maurice in high esteem. In 1998 Maurice was dramatically – but briefly – dismissed as chief executive of BARLA, causing a storm of indignation among its members. Ken Arthurson, in my opinion, was, along with Maurice, the only rugby league administrator to come out of the Super League war with their reputation intact. Ken was at that time the immediate past chairman of the Australian Rugby League and International Board. He was so incensed at Maurice's treatment that he wrote an open letter, which included the following: "Based on my experience of more than 50 years in Rugby League as a player, coach and administrator, I have met few people possessing [such] dedication and passion for the sport of Rugby League as Maurice Oldroyd. His unswerving loyalty and his determination for the success of that association [BARLA], is reflected in the enormous increase in the number of teams in amateur Rugby League in Britain during his term of office. During my term as Chairman of the International Rugby League Board, I will say quite categorically that nobody contributed more to International development than Maurice... Mr

Oldroyd is a man of the highest possible integrity and Rugby League can ill afford to lose people of his calibre." (The full letter is included as an appendix to this book).

Leaving aside Deputy Speakers of the House of Commons and former chairmen of the Australian Rugby League, it is interesting to observe how the average rugby league follower regards Maurice. Going to an amateur match with Maurice can be both a pleasure and a pain, especially if you actually want to watch the game. Everybody seems to know him. If you accompany him round the field, he is constantly stopping or being stopped by folk who have something to tell him or who need to be told something. It is a bit like a medieval royal progress. The distractions mean that the game itself becomes peripheral and it becomes a heck of a job to keep track of the score. My advice is to let him walk round on his own. Of course, this is all part of Maurice's networking obsession. It is not unusual for Maurice to take in three games on a Saturday afternoon if the venues are close enough.

Maurice has immersed his life in amateur rugby league. He has served BARLA from its genesis and for that the whole sport should be grateful. Apart from the foundation of the game in 1895, it is arguable that the creation and progress of BARLA has been the most important development in rugby league in the 20th century. Without the drive and initiative of the BARLA pioneers from the 1970s onwards rugby league would never have developed in Britain to the extent it did. It may well now be past its prime, as inevitably other sectors of the game grow and reduce BARLA's relative importance. Nonetheless, its significance as an engine driving up the numbers participating in rugby league, enhancing the environment in which those numbers play and bringing public money into the sport, can never be overestimated. Nor should the massive contribution of Maurice Oldroyd to the sport of rugby league ever be forgotten.

**Robert Gate**
**April 2014**


**Thank you**

Maurice Oldroyd and London League Publications Ltd would like to thank the following people who helped with this book:
Robert Gate – who spent many hours with Maurice working on the manuscript and preparing it for publication. It took around six years, and without Robert's contribution this book would not have happened.
Everyone who supplied photos or gave permission for their use.
Steve McCarthy for designing the cover.
The staff of Charlesworth Press for printing the book.

# Contents

David Oxley CBE and Maurice
at the 2013 Albert Goldthorpe Awards ceremony.
(Photo: David Williams, rlphotos.com)

# 1. In the beginning: 1935 to 1950

Birkby is a nice, posh area of Huddersfield. Nowadays a house there can fetch up to £5 million. I was born there, but there was nothing posh about our house in Birkby Lodge Road. It was a back-to-back in a block of eight houses, which were split in two by a passage. We shared an outside lavatory with our neighbours. We just had one room on the ground floor, plus a cellar-head which served as the kitchen. We had a tin bath in the cellar and the oven was also down there. The cellar was stone flagged, so it was pretty primitive and there was a sectioned off area which served as the coal bunker. We had a bit of a garden on three sides, but all I can remember of it was that there was a rose bush which clambered up the toilet wall. The view we had was not really of the picture-box variety either. Birkby Lodge Road looked out on Hopkinson's Valves, one of Huddersfield's major employers. I remember clearly that, when the workers clocked off, it was just like a flood-tide of humanity as they streamed across Blacker Road. We had two bedrooms and an attic, where I kept my press cuttings about Fartown in a tin box.

Fartown was the name of Huddersfield Rugby League Club's ground, as well as the nickname the supporters called the team. Some of them still do, even though it is more than 20 years since they played their last game at the old ground before moving on to become the Giants at the new McAlpine Stadium, which in turn has now been renamed the Galpharm. To a lot of people though, Huddersfield RLFC will always remain Fartown. Anyway, Fartown was an obsession for me for a long time. The ground was just down the road from our house. Birkby Lodge Road led into Blacker Road, which in turn led to Fartown.

One of our neighbours was Frank Stamper, a Cumbrian forward who had played for Fartown in the days after the First World War, when many of the players from the gloriously successful Team of All the Talents of pre-war days were still winning trophies under Harold Wagstaff. Our coal was always delivered by another of that team, Douglas Clark. He carried a hundredweight sack in each hand. He barely fitted down the passageway. Clark was another Cumbrian, one of the greatest forwards the game has known and a world champion wrestler. He has now been inducted into the Rugby League Hall of

Fame. My granddad, who worked on the railways, would often have a bit of a friendly wrestle with Clark. He must have been potty!

Another Cumbrian was his partner in the coal delivery business – Stan Pepperell, from Seaton, an international scrum-half, who also played for Huddersfield, but was a lot younger than Duggie. The three Pepperell brothers all played international rugby league.

The Fiddes family lived just nearby in Armitage Road. Alex Fiddes, a Scot, was a brilliant centre and was captain of Huddersfield for about 12 years until he retired in 1947. His sons Billy, Ian and Jack were familiar to me. Ian was a good enough rugby union player to play in a Scottish trial. Another two lads who went a long way lived in Tanfield Road. One was Raymond Haywood, who signed as a professional for Fartown and played in the centre against Wakefield Trinity at Wembley in 1962. The other was Dennis Broadbent, who captained Bradford Northern in their last game before the club collapsed in 1963. His father was the doorman at the George Hotel, the birthplace of rugby league. With all those rugby connections I suppose I was predestined to become involved in the game.

I had a happy childhood. I was an only child. We didn't have much money, but that didn't seem to matter. Ours was a typically working class household. My father Harry was Huddersfield born and bred. His sister, my auntie Alice, later came to live in the same block of houses that we lived in. Dad was a jovial type of man, a bit of a character really. He had a nice personality and was a bit of a comedian, especially in the company of his mates. He was never unemployed, although he changed jobs a lot. He mostly worked as a labourer in the textile mills or engineering works. His last position was as an odd job man at Haywood and Williams Glaziers at the bottom of Blacker Road. Although he was a manual worker he was not a strong man. He failed his medical for army service in the Second World War. I think he served in the Home Guard, however. He certainly had a helmet resembling an ARP helmet, although I don't think he was ever an ARP warden. His idea of a good time was a trip across the road the Horse Shoe pub for a pint of mild, a packet of Woodbines, sixpence each way on Lester Piggott at 10–1 on and a game of dominoes. Needless to say, he was a Fartown supporter and used to organise trips to away games from the Horse Shoe.

My mother – Mam – came from Briestfield, near Dewsbury, which explained why there was always a copy of *The Dewsbury Reporter* in the house and why I have such a lot of relatives in the Dewsbury and Flockton areas. She was called Amy and her maiden name was Fisher. She was born in 1901, which made her a couple of years older than Dad. Mam was a small woman, very even tempered and presented a distinct contrast to the flamboyant nature of my father. I would say she was the anchor of our family. Mam had a couple of sisters – Elsie, who married a farmer, who lived opposite Shuttle Eye Colliery, and Helen, who married a miner. She also had a brother John, who eventually ended up living in Blackpool.

Mam sometimes worked part-time in the mills and did a few hours office cleaning, but she was never in full-time employment, at least not after I appeared in the world. Working class mothers in those days hardly ever worked full-time. I remember she did a bit of domestic work for a German family, the Mannheims, who lived at the top end of Birkby. I think she must have been a very frugal house-keeper. Once, I remember, she came into some sort of family legacy. It might have been a few hundred pounds, or maybe not even that much. Whatever it was, it seemed like a lot at the time but Mam made sure that Dad did not get anywhere near it. Although I was an only child, Mam actively encouraged other kids to visit the house and we had a lot of fun one way and another. Dad enjoyed playing cards with the kids and delighted in showing them how to cheat. Mam made sure that I went to church. We used to go to the Baptist church at first. I have an idea that she was on the ladies' committee there. Later, however, we transferred our allegiance to St John's, which was Church of England. I joined their Wolf Cubs, but never graduated to the Scouts, largely because I became so engrossed in rugby league.

Our extended family seemed to be quite close. I remember visiting cousins at Flockton and overnighting there. We would go on holidays every summer, usually to Bridlington, sometimes to Scarborough and also to Blackpool, where Uncle John had taken up residence, although we only saw him a couple of times while we were there. We would go by bus, as we never had a car and train travel was probably too expensive. We would often go with auntie Helen and my cousins Marjorie, Colin, Selwyn and Keith. Keith became a butcher. Selwyn was killed in a pit accident at Shuttle Eye, where Colin also worked. When

3

we went to Bridlington we would lodge in the Old Town. We had to buy our own food and the landlady would cook it for us.

Once we ended up in Blackpool in the middle of winter. I think I must have been 13 years old and returned home from playing rugby as usual one Saturday morning. Straightaway I noticed a funny smell in the house and one of the neighbours was waiting to tell me that Mam had been rushed to Huddersfield Infirmary. She had been cleaning a clock at the cellar head. She remembered that someone once told her that paraffin was good for cleaning clocks. Maybe it is but Mam must have not taken in the details. She had put the clock in a pan with some paraffin and heated it up. The paraffin boiled over and flames shot up. Mam's instinct was to get the pan out of the house. She threw it down the outside steps and then fell down them. She ended up in hospital for several weeks, her arms and face badly burnt. I remember that the Infirmary staff covered her burns with gentian violets. When she came home no mirrors were allowed in the house. However, she made a remarkable recovery. The only legacies of the accident were a scar on her forearm and very small scar above her upper lip. She obviously had good healing qualities, which I am sure I have inherited.

It was decided that she needed some proper rest and recuperation so the three of us decamped for Blackpool. This was in December. We did not stay with uncle John though; we lodged in a boarding house. My main memory of the period was going with Dad to Bloomfield Road to watch Huddersfield Town play Blackpool. I had hardly ever seen Town play soccer because I was a dyed-in-the-wool Fartowner. I was thrilled though because I got to see the fantastic Blackpool and England forwards, Stanley Matthews and Stan Mortenson.

I was born on 19 November, 1935 at Fern Street Hospital. So when the Second World War ended I was getting on for 10. By then I was aware that there was indeed a war going on. When I was about six I remember the air raid sirens going off and we had to vacate the house. Most air raid shelters were red-brick constructions with concrete roofs but ours was the passage between the two blocks of four houses. Steel doors had been bolted on to hard wood frames at each end of the passage, with the steel on the outside. There was some sort of corrugated roofing covering the passage. I recall we used to pile into the passage with cushions and blankets and wait for the all clear signal. One night a lad called Jack Broadbent came to visit our house. In the black-out, it was so dark that he walked straight into the steel door! I think the nearest we came to being bombed was when a land-mine was dropped at Lindley, near Pat Martin's Mill, but it did not explode.

I do remember watching the progress of the war at the cinema through *British Gaumont News* and *Pathe News* reels and listening to the BBC news bulletins on our wireless. I certainly enjoyed VE and VJ Days. That was mostly because of the street parties. Ours were held in Tanfield Road, where the Haywoods and Broadbents lived. The trestle tables were pushed together and ran the whole length of the street, a wonderful sight for a nine year-old. I also went to Huddersfield to see Winston Churchill, who must have been doing a celebratory tour sometime after VE Day. I remember straining to see him on tip-toe as he addressed the crowd from a dais between the railway station and the George Hotel. He got a really tumultuous reception.

As a child I was not strong. Maybe in that respect I inherited Dad's genes. Later in life Mam told me I had had to have two six months periods off school. The first one was apparently because of the after-effects of the measles. I do remember having to attend a clinic in Ramsden Street, near the town hall, for sun ray treatment. We had to queue up for the treatment and get a card signed when we had received it. I had the proverbial bad chest and have been a bit asthmatic all my life. I still carry an atomiser now.

Before I had been old enough for school Mam had put me into clogs, so she could hear me in the passage outside our house. Later on I was given some very sturdy, waterproof clogs with inch high heels. I loved those clogs because I could charge up and down shallow streams and look for tiddlers without getting my feet wet.

My education began at Birkby County School in Blacker Road in the first year of the war. We had no uniforms, but I recall we all had gasmasks, which we kept in little boxes. One of my earliest memories of school is the arrival of a group of evacuees from London. They all wore medium grey shirts with red collars and piping. Huddersfield must have seemed very strange to them. Another memory which has stuck with me was my grandmother coming down to school with me and smacking someone who had hit me. The headmaster at Birkby was Mr Mallalieu and he ran a very sporty school. I really enjoyed my time there, particularly playing for the school rugby team. I can remember being thrilled to play against Beaumont School at Fartown one Saturday morning.

Aged 11, having passed the 11-plus, I moved on to Hillhouse Secondary School. When I arrived there it was still known as Central School and was in the process of becoming a grammar school, although it was never called that. Mam decided to send me there rather than Royd's Hall, Almondbury Grammar or Huddersfield College because it was nearer home. In fact it was only about 400 yards from Fartown, which suited me down to the ground. Eventually Hillhouse Secondary merged with Huddersfield College. The school actually shared a playground with the neighbouring Hillhouse Council School, which took both boys and girls. Our school was a boys only establishment. I think that the fact that we were an exclusively boys school gave us something of an advantage when it came to sport. We wore maroon blazers and were divided into four houses – Campbell, Granville, Scott and Windsor. I was a Windsor boy. I remember that our colour was white but I forget the other house colours. The headmaster was Harry Armitage and his deputy was Joss Whitwam – there were two pretty typical Huddersfield names! Both were getting on and grey haired. The teachers wore gowns, so they had clearly already adopted the grammar school ethos.

Quite a few famous rugby league players had been Hillhouse boys. Probably the most famous was Stanley Moorhouse. Moorhouse was a member of the Team of All the Talents, which dominated the sport just before the First World War, and he played left wing to Harold Wagstaff. He won all the game's honours, including a tour to Australasia in 1914. Frank Royston was on the wing when Huddersfield won the Championship in 1930 and played stand-off for Yorkshire in 1934. Whether either of them actually attended my old school is a mystery to me, but I do know that when I arrived at Hillhouse rugby league was not on the curriculum.

We played soccer to start with, but Bill Waterhouse, a science master and very nice man, introduced rugby league, probably after a year or so of my arrival. Later on Bob Hesford joined the school staff. He had a very cynical and sarcastic line in wit. He took PE, but did not appear to want to! Instead he used to spend a lot of the time getting the boys to bowl at him in cricket practice. He seemed to be a sort of floating teacher. We could not pigeon hole him although he did teach some geography. He was, however, something of a celebrity because he had been Huddersfield Town's goalkeeper at Wembley in 1938. That was the year when Preston North End beat us by a penalty in the last 30 seconds of extra time. Bob Hesford was beaten by George Mutch's shot, which went in off the underside of the cross-bar. What a hero he would have been if he had saved it.

In a funny way it reminds me of Don Fox's misfortune at the rugby league final at Wembley in 1968, although Bob could hardly be blamed for failing to save a penalty. It is certainly one of English football's most famous and controversial goals. Pity it had to be scored against Huddersfield Town though. Bob Hesford's son Iain became a goalie with Blackpool and another of his sons, Steve, had a successful career as a full-back with Warrington, becoming one of the best goalkickers rugby league has ever seen.

Another Hillhouse lad who made his name in rugby league was Frank 'Spanky' Dyson. Frank, who was about four years older than me, had gone to Hillhouse Council School and lived very close by. Although he had already left school and was training to be a motor-mechanic, he could not resist coming into the school playgrounds to play football with us. Being older, bigger and stronger, he sometimes fairly terrorised us in his big working boots and overalls. Once he got so mad with one of the lads that he chased after him and threw a screw-driver at him. Thank goodness, he missed. Frank went on to become a tremendous full-back and goalkicker for Fartown. He broke all sorts of records, played at Wembley in 1962 and represented Yorkshire and Great Britain.

I was happy at Hillhouse. I made plenty of friends, thoroughly enjoyed the sport and learned the value of discipline. There was not a lot of physical punishment although it certainly had its place. For example, I remember 'Zak' Zacharias, a small chap who was a senior master, giving pupils a quick clip round the ears if they were acting up in the corridors. We also had an art teacher who had rather cruelly been dubbed 'Squint-eyed Syd'. We used to sing a ditty which went, "Squint-eyed Syd from Scarborough town. One eye up, one eye down. One eye green, one eye brown." We all thought it was funny when he would say to an errant boy, "I am looking at you now, boy. Stand-up!" Because we couldn't tell who he was looking at, we would all stand up. He would get his own back though by inviting miscreants to his "Oxo club". His victim would be told to fetch a huge T-square, which was kept in the art room and Syd would chalk OXO onto the cross of the T-square. He would then instruct the boy to bend over, making sure his trousers were stretched tight and proceed to emboss OXO on his bottom. The class watched this performance with a strange mixture of trepidation and mirth.

Then there was the woodwork teacher, who because he actually did have a wooden leg, was inevitably nicknamed 'Peg-leg'. The tables in the woodwork room were arranged in a U-shape. When we wound him up enough he would chase a boy into the neck of the U but would be unable to lay hands on him if the lad was quick enough to vault over the tables.

Apart from such pantomimic interludes, my obsession with rugby was the main focus of my time at Hillhouse. We had a pretty good team and I was fortunate enough to be a member of a side which won the Hoyle Cup, Huddersfield Schools' knock-out competition for under–15s, three years in a row. Being small, I naturally gravitated to the scrum-half position. I was a bit of a schemer, a good handler and I made a lot of interceptions. I also loved tackling the big lads and particularly enjoyed crash-tackling – maybe I was stupid! I broke my collar-bone three times. The first, I recall, was in a game against Moldgreen. My main worry was when we got to the hospital when I asked the master who had gone with me "How will they get my shirt off, sir?" He told me not to worry: "They have probably done it before".

We certainly had some good players – most of them seemed to be sons of local businessmen. Max Ramsden was a really good hooker. He went on to become an England amateur international player. On one memorable occasion we beat Crossley and Porter School in Halifax by about 48–0 in a Yorkshire Cup game and we were all full of ourselves the day after at school.

Bill Waterhouse had a shock for Max though, when he went over the game with us in the science lab. Max had scored a hat-trick of tries and was quietly beaming away to himself waiting for Bill's appraisal of his performance. He was taken aback when Bill bawled, "Ramsden, you are a hooker. You are there to get the ball for your team-mates. It is not for hookers to score hat-tricks. We have got two perfectly good wingers. Come out here! Bend over!"

I don't suppose Max was very happy about that, but Bill was right about the wingers. Neville Pearson played for Yorkshire Schools and the other winger, Gerald Walker, signed for Hull Kingston Rovers. Tragically, Gerald later committed suicide. Another winger I played with at school, who was in the year below me was Norman Field, a really powerful lad. Norman went on to play for Batley and Featherstone and played a test match for Britain against Australia at Wembley in 1963. Mam had a real soft spot for Norman and used to give him pigeon pie when he came round to our house. In later life Norman and his brother Reggie had a garage business down on Bradford Road in Huddersfield, but Norman eventually ended up as an hotelier in Torquay.

Another pupil who did well was Geoff 'Slim' Smith, a prop. Slim was a year older than me and he was massive. I think he was already about 14 stones and he was a good goalkicker. When he was aged 17 he signed for Keighley. One of his earliest games for them was at Fartown against Huddersfield in November 1951 and we all went to watch him. I think he was a bit upstaged though because Lionel Cooper, the Australian Fartown winger, ran in 10 tries and Huddersfield won 48–3. Slim was a tremendous swimmer and used to win practically everything at the school swimming galas. He could also throw a cricket ball further than anyone else at school.

Alec's Fiddes's son Bill, a year younger than me, was in the side too. Like me, he was a half-back. He later played for many years for Huddersfield RU club with his brother Ian. We had yet another talented half-back in Ernie Clare, who was a year older than me and, I would say, a better player than me.

For the last season and a half of my time at Hillhouse I captained the rugby league team. As I said, we won the Hoyle Cup three years running. The finals were played at Leeds Road Playing Fields, I think. We played against schools such as Hillhouse Council, St Patrick's, St Joseph's, Beaumont Street and Moldgreen. We beat St Patrick's in one of the finals and they had some tough boys. Peter Ramsden, who won the Lance Todd Trophy when Huddersfield beat St Helens in 1953, was on the losing side that day. They also had a future ABA light-middle weight champion in John Cunningham who won his title in 1957. Moldgreen had a couple of stars too in Charlie and Eddie Williams. Eddie also became an ABA champion and later fought Yolande Pompey, who lost a world light-heavyweight title fight to Archie Moore. Pompey was a bit too good for Eddie though. A day or two after his loss to Pompey I saw Eddie in Huddersfield. Even though I was 20 yards away I could not miss his two beautiful black eyes.

I have still got my three winners' medals from those Hoyle Cup finals, although I did not actually play in the third final. That was because I had left school at Christmas but as I had played in some of the earlier rounds I was entitled to a medal. Perhaps our best achievement, though, was reaching the Yorkshire Cup final one season. Unfortunately, we lost to a school from Kirkstall in Leeds, coached by Ken Dalby. Ken was manager of Leeds when they won the Rugby League Championship for the first time in 1961. The following season we got to the semi-finals.

I also remember playing against Peter Ramsden, who won the Lance Todd Trophy when he played for Huddersfield in the 1953 Challenge Cup Final.

At school and my youth club, we played 'touch and pass' but then in the holidays we played with tackling on the grass in the park. I had a friend who was great at 'touch and pass' but didn't fancy rugby league with full-on tackling. At school we also played a game of throwing a rugby ball over a badminton net, which taught us how to float passes.

We also had a pretty successful soccer side at Hillhouse but I did not play for the school, although I did turn out for my house team. Away from school I played soccer as a right winger for Birkby Civic Youth Club in the local Red Triangle League.

I played for the school cricket team, opening the batting and doing a bit of bowling. The highlight of my cricketing career would have been when we reached a local final against Stile Common School at Primrose Hill. Ken Taylor, who became a Yorkshire and England opener and was a top class footballer with Huddersfield Town, was in the Stile Common team. Ken had a good opening partner in Brian Stott for Yorkshire and later opened the innings with Geoff Boycott. As a footballer he was a very hard tackler, but not dirty. He is now quite a famous artist.

I also did a bit of boxing at school and joined a boxing club in Huddersfield town centre on New Street, opposite Woolworths. I was not there for long though. On the whole I decided I would be safer on the rugby field. I have always retained an interest in boxing though and regard it as the ultimate sporting challenge.

Huddersfield had a network of civic youth clubs based at council schools. There were such clubs at Lockwood, Moldgreen, Netherton and Oakes and quite a few others, including Birkby which I joined. They were very supportive of sporting activities and at Birkby we got a lot of rugby league input from the sport's personalities like Alec Fiddes and Australian full-back Johnny Hunter, one of my all-time favourite players. They taught us a lot, particularly in ball-handling skills, and we were indoctrinated into good habits by them. Birkby was an area which seemed to produce sportsmen and I share something of a distinction with two of my contemporaries, Ian Fiddes and Raymond Haywood. We all captained Huddersfield schoolboys – Ian at soccer, Raymond at cricket and myself at rugby league.

Not long before I left we got a new headmaster, who introduced rugby union to the school. He steered quite a few boys to Huddersfield Old Boys at Waterloo and I spent some time there playing for the Colts. However, I was too keen on rugby league to take rugby union seriously. After a while I was instrumental in forming a rugby league team of old boys from school and we played as Old Centralians at Fieldhouse Lane, behind Leeds Road Playing Fields. We played mostly against youth clubs and, I seem to recall, the Sea Cadets, and in our first full season ran eventual winners Honley close for the title. Maybe we should have ground-shared with the Sea Cadets, as we played next to the canal and there was a lot of fun retrieving the ball when it ended up in the water, which it often did.

In one game we scored 135 points against Woodhouse and our full-back, Jack Ellam, grabbed 51 points from a try and 24 goals. Eventually Old Centralians folded as members were called up for National service or left through other circumstances. I joined Woodhouse – more as a challenge than anything, I suppose, and was pleased that the team managed to show a good deal of improvement from the days when Old Centralians rattled up those 135 points.

Lionel Cooper and Johnny Hunter (Courtesy Michael O'Hare)

Left: Pat Devery with the Championship trophy in 1949.
Right: Frank 'Spanky' Dyson. (Both courtesy David Gronow)

# 2. The world of work

Schooldays over, I turned my thoughts to the world of work. Hillhouse School had been pretty good with careers guidance. They arranged for boys to visit the big local engineering and textile firms and other organisations such as *The Huddersfield Examiner*. My strong point at school was maths and it seemed logical to train for accountancy. I got an interview at Wheawill and Sudworth's Chartered Accountants and landed a post as audit clerk. As the world of chartered accountancy was strictly hierarchical, that meant I was at the very bottom – basically the office-boy – but that's where everyone started in those days. The offices were in Westgate near the railway station and the firm is still going strong. When BARLA was formed, its offices were only about 100 yards from Wheawill and Sudworth's, so I did not get too far, when all is said and done. One advantage of work was its proximity to Birkby because I was always able to walk home for dinner.

Charlie Wheawill and Elijah Sudworth were the two senior partners. One of my jobs was to fill Elijah's fountain pens – talk about responsibility! Anyway, I learned that accountancy was a great preparation for life. I always considered the profession to be a sort of flexible tool. Accountants get everywhere – and so do sportsmen. Edwin Lister, who was head of a section and later became a partner at the firm, was a goalkicking full-back for the Huddersfield Old Boys rugby union team. Peter Dibb, just a year older than me and an articled clerk, was a good hockey player with Honley and an excellent cricketer. He played hockey until he was aged 61, and retired from cricket, aged 76, in 2009.

Edwin Lister requisitioned me to send out the team selection post-cards to the Old Boys' Colts players – one of the perks of having juniors like me to call upon to do their bidding, I suppose. Mind you, there were benefits. One day he gave me the keys to his car boot and told me to go and have a look and see if there was anything I wanted. The boot was full of pairs of rugby boots and I helped myself to a couple of pairs. That was a bit like finding treasure for someone like me. Boots were expensive.

I enjoyed working at Wheawill and Sudworth's. My starting pay was £2 and 10 shillings (£2.50) a week, paid monthly. There was always a large white fiver in my pay packet, something I'll never forget. Another abiding memory is the annual Bank Holiday staff outing to Scarborough, when we would play cricket or rounders on the beach. The senior partners did not accompany us on the bus, however.

Apart from topping up Elijah's fountain pens, I used to deliver post to town centre businesses, was responsible for the petty cash book and manned the switchboard, complete with headphones – the whole works. After a year and now rejoicing in the title of junior audit clerk, I was despatched with audit teams into the wider world to places like the Imperial Hotel, Blackpool, Beeches Chocolates at Preston and the Readicut Wool Company at Horbury, Wakefield.

Nearer to home, I was privileged to enter through the portals of the Borough Club, which was opposite Huddersfield Town Hall in Ramsden Street and adjacent to the offices of the *Huddersfield Examiner*. In effect the Borough Club was the power base of the town. Huddersfield at this period had many millionaires, possibly more per capita than anywhere apart from London. This was what people said about Huddersfield at that time. The Borough Club was one of the places where Elijah was to be found and I had to carry his pens backwards and forwards to him to get cheques, forms and letters signed. It was a very useful and informative way of finding out how power operates. I was fascinated.

All the mill owners and the town's movers and shakers frequented the Borough Club, so I got to know who was who in Huddersfield's highest circles. For my seniors it was a place where business could be gained, as all mills had their own accountants. Among our major clients were firms like Taylor and Lodge, William Thompson's Fine Cloths and Longwood Finishing Company. We also audited Huddersfield Choral Society, Woodsome Hall Golf Club and Huddersfield Golf Club, where John Fallon was the pro. He captained the Ryder Cup team in 1963.

Of course, I was only an interested observer, just a junior clerk, fresh out of school. We did not take 'O' Levels (now GCSEs) at Hillhouse, so I really had no qualifications. I went to Huddersfield Technical College a couple of nights a week in order to study for the Chartered Accountants Preliminary Examination and took 'O' Levels in geography and mathematics. From leaving school until I was called up for National Service at 18, I remained at Wheawill and Sudworth's wondering what life was going to throw at me. I do not think I was overly ambitious, but I did want to get on.

14

Huddersfield Rugby League team 1948–49:
Northern Rugby League Champions.

Hillhouse School team 1950–51.
Maurice is on the front row, one in from the left.

Like other lads of my age, I had developed the normal appetites, such as a liking for female company. I was a regular at the local dance venues on Saturday nights – Huddersfield Town Hall, Cambridge Road Baths and the Masonic Hall. I was still rugby mad and had the odd trial at Fartown – I played a few games for the 'A' team as an amateur– but I knew I was not going to be good enough to play professionally. Besides, in those days, particularly at Fartown, if you weren't an Australian you hadn't much chance of getting anywhere. A lot of people would say that's true of rugby league in general now!

Soon enough I would have more to think about than Fartown's fortunes, although they would always be something of a preoccupation for me. This was the era of National Service and I got my call-up papers a few days after my 18th birthday. Apprentices could delay their entry into the forces until they were 21. Although I knew that I was going to get called up, I really did not think I would pass the medical because of my history of asthma. However, I was passed A1 and was lucky because I got into the RAF, which is what I wanted. Bert Thornton, who would be my best man, ended up in Singapore with the RAF, but I did not get anything like as far from home.

Not long after Christmas 1953, I became a fully paid up member of the Royal Air Force on 28 bob (£1.40) a week or four shillings a day. I received a travel warrant for RAF Cardington in Bedfordshire. We only spent a few days there. They kitted us out there on the basis that "everything fitted where it touched".

The routine was: rise at 6.30am, breakfast at 7, on parade at 7.45. Memories of marching around in the dark flood back, wearing big, heavy boots and doing a good impression of the Gestapo arriving. Then suddenly we were dispersed to all parts of the country. I ended up at RAF Hednesford, near Cannock Chase for about six weeks of square bashing. I actually quite enjoyed it. Some people were absolutely petrified by the experience, but I had a somewhat cynical attitude. Although I was never a troublemaker I retained a sense of bolshiness. Don't get me wrong; I respected authority, but I could see the amusing side of our situation despite the insistence on discipline. I think National Service did me good. It placed me in a different environment and I met people from all walks of life, who I would otherwise never have met.

Serving my country! National Service at RAF Hednesford.
Maurice is third from the left in the middle row.

It was a form of education in many ways. At RAF Hednesford I came across Sergeant Dai Rees, who was a Physical Training Instructor (PTI). He was a scrum-half for Belle Vue Rangers, a Welsh international and certainly made sure we were fit.

From RAF Hednesford I was sent to Middle Wallop – what a name – on Salisbury Plain. RAF Middle Wallop was a RADAR station then, although it is now an Army-RAF museum. I had been sent on a four week course to become a fighter plotter. It was a skill that has stood me in good stead in the administrative and political world of rugby league and life in general. It really was like the old war films where they push model planes about on a big board. Replete with head-phones, we monitored all planes, especially those considered to be hostile. After that course I was despatched to Hack Green, near Nantwich in Cheshire. It was a beautiful little village and I enjoyed the rugby union and cricket we played there. The RAF station no longer exists, although there is a museum on the site. The neighbouring villages of Nether Wallop and Over Wallop were well known for their water cress beds.

While I was at Nantwich I was sent on another course to RAF Wharton, near Blackpool and St Anne's. Some of the first turbine-powered planes to break the sound barrier were made there by English Electric. Not that I ever got into a plane while I was in the RAF. We did get photographed in front of a Spitfire, though. I think that was more or less compulsory; we posed like a rugby team in front of one. The first time I actually flew in an aeroplane was soon after leaving the RAF, when I went to Spain on holiday with a few mates.

I was sent on another short course to RAF Uxbridge, famous for being Winston Churchill's command centre, but mostly I spent my National Service at RAF Hack Green. I played scrum-half for Crewe and Nantwich Rugby Union club regularly and was in the station's cricket team. They assumed that anyone from Yorkshire must be good at the game, but really I was only a modest performer.

Our Commanding Officer was very keen on sport, particularly cricket, and he was thrilled when we got to the final of the AOC competition for RAF stations. I remember him telling me we needed a fast bowler and he would have to do something about it. A couple of days later a bloke called Jones appeared from St Anne's with a rucksack on his back to report for duty. Needless to say, he was a fast bowler. It is funny, but I cannot remember whether we won or lost that final. I do remember that for once I got a good score of 40 odd and that at one point we were about 90 for 1, but did not reach 200 all out. Once we had a tennis competition and I reached the semi-finals. My opponent was the Commanding Officer, so I made sure I lost.

At Nantwich there was a lad who was a keen rugby league fan. His brother was a director at Leigh and said I should go for a trial there. His brother then arranged for me to play for Leigh 'A' against Wigan 'A' at Kirkhall Lane. Jimmy Featherstone, the test forward, and Don Platt, a pretty good full-back, were in the Wigan ranks. I had a steady game and tackled well, but did not make any breaks. Leigh did not pursue me any further, so it confirmed what I already suspected – that I would never make a professional rugby league player. Never mind.

Life in the RAF was not so bad once you got used to it. We got regular weekend leaves and I became quite expert at hitch-hiking back home from Nantwich. Returning was different. We used to converge on Leeds, where RAF coaches picked us up and took us to the various stations.

RAF Nantwich Cricket team.
Maurice is third from the right in the front row.

RAF demob do at the Cheshire Cat pub.

I recall we used to wait for the coach in Jim Windsor's club and it left about 11pm. We used to listen to the Top 20 on Radio Luxemburg, and returned to our stations in the early hours.

There were some interesting people doing National Service in my time at Hack Green. Among them was Peter Goodright, who became a popular impressionist on radio and television. Another, whose name escapes me, became the jazz musician Johnny Dankworth's agent, but the most famous was Keith Barron, the actor, who appeared in all sorts of wonderful productions on radio, television, stage and screen. I still see him on television today.

All things come to an end and so did my RAF career. There were a couple of good demob bashes at two local hostelries, the *Church's Mansion* and the *Cheshire Cat* and suddenly I was back in civilian life. I believe that spell in the forces was a great learning curve for many young men. My only regret was that I had been unable to get leave for the 1954 Odsal replay between Halifax and Warrington. That was one occasion I would love to have attended and my presence would have pushed the official attendance up 102,570.

In recent years a National Service (RAF) Association has been founded. On 25 June, 2006, over half a century after my demob, I attended a reunion parade at the RAF Museum Cosford. The parade and march past, accompanied by the Central Band of the Royal Air Force, was a grand affair, held under the tender care of former 1950s Drill Instructors. There were 480 men on parade, 1,096 at the museum and another 1,500 spectators.

At the proverbial three score years and 10, perhaps I had come full circle.

# 3. Fartown and Huddersfield Town

I am not quite sure exactly when my love affair with Fartown began, but it must have been when I was aged around nine. I can remember that we used to go to watch *Flash Gordon* at the Regent Cinema on Bradford Road on Saturdays and would pass the ground on the way. The first glimpse I had of the posts through the gates made me think that that they were for high jumping. Heavens knows what made me think that but it seemed logical at the time.

It is odd that I cannot recall the first game I saw at Fartown, but I can remember that Aston Villa in their distinctive claret and blue shirts were the first opposition I saw take on Huddersfield Town at their Leeds Road ground. While I was not as passionate about soccer as rugby, I did appreciate great players when I saw them. The best Town players I saw were Peter Doherty and Dennis Law. Doherty was just brilliant and Law was so sharp, competitive and decisive. I remember Law and Kevin McHale making their debuts as a wing and inside forward pairing when both were only 16 years old. I also admired Ray Wilson as a full-back and will never forget the day he and Stanley Matthews took each other on. It ended in an honourable draw, I would say. Wilson, who became an undertaker, was, of course, destined to become a World Cup winner with England in 1966. Local boy done good; you could certainly say.

The period immediately after the war was a wonderful sporting era. I always say sport civilised people after the war. I genuinely consider myself lucky to have been around in that period. Sport seemed to envelop me and my friends. When we were not playing we were watching. When we were not watching, we were listening to it on the wireless. My best mate, Bert Thornton, and I used to listen to the big boxing matches featuring fighters like Freddie Mills, Bruce Woodcock, Jack London and Dick Richardson. I can still recall Barrington Dalby and Raymond Glendenning doing the commentaries. I can also remember John Arlott reporting on the cricket and staying up into the early hours of the morning for the Ashes broadcasts from Australia.

Summer holidays, all six or seven weeks of them, would find us playing rugby league or other games, morning, noon and night on the various recreation grounds and in local parks. On Sunday mornings up at Oakes Recreation Ground, Huddersfield Town manager Bill Shankly joining in with the kids' soccer games and dropping youngsters as if they were playing league football. Peter Todd, a real hard case of a centre who played for Halifax at Wembley in 1954, was just as ruthless. Sometimes, we used to play soccer or rugby at Highfields, near Greenhead Park; he would join in and practically hack us to death. Peter was a lovely man off the field and a regular church-goer. I once saw him absolutely smash Dick Cracknell, our international winger, at Fartown. They took Dick off in a real daze. After the game I saw Peter go down into the dressing-rooms and greet Dick with a most solicitous enquiry about his mother's and father's health. Years later, I asked Peter how he could reconcile his fiery nature on the pitch with his calm demeanour off it, but he couldn't. He said it was just how life was.

Huddersfield had a wonderful rugby league team in this period. It played glorious rugby – probably the most attractive I have ever witnessed. It was a team of all nations – there were English, Scottish, Welsh, Irish, Australian, New Zealand and South African players – and many of them would have been stars in any era. At the time I do not think that we realised just how privileged we were to see such a brilliant group of players. I realise this now because hindsight is a wonderful gift. What's more, access to this fabulous form of entertainment was free. Schoolchildren were not charged to get into Fartown. We stood in the 'hen pen' behind the posts at the scoreboard end of the ground.

Some of the crowds we got in those days were absolutely huge. One of my earliest memories is of attending a Challenge Cup semi-final between Leeds and Wakefield Trinity in 1947 when the ground record crowd of over 35,000 at Fartown was set. In my teens I graduated to being a helper on the scoreboard. I cannot describe how fantastic a view it was from high up, looking straight down the field, when there was a full house at Fartown.

Mam's favourite Fartowner was Billy Banks, the little Welsh scrum-half. She came to watch me play in an evening knock-out competition at the Sands House pub in Crosland Moor. Teams were allowed to field a couple of professionals and Billy, golden hair and a real star, joined in. He was bundled over the touch-line and crashed into Mam, knocking her over. She never stopped talking about it. My favourites were not Welsh. They were the Australian trio of Devery, Cooper and Hunter. In

May 2012, I was one of the guest speakers at the launch of a book, *Three Fartown Aussies*, about them by David Gronow.

Pat Devery, a good goalkicker, was an absolutely top class centre with explosive pace. He had played stand-off for Australia in all three Ashes tests in 1946, but formed a brilliant centre-wing partnership with Lionel Cooper at Fartown. Cooper was so big and strong that he was a nightmare for opposing wings. He scored 441 tries in eight years and Brian Bevan and he were practically unstoppable in different ways as wingers for the Other Nationalities international team. I'll never forget how the ball used to ripple through the Huddersfield back-line – Banks to Pepperell to Devery. When it got to Pat there would be a great roar of expectation as his hands prepared to send the ball on to Cooper. Then it was heaven help the other side.

For sheer entertainment on a football field, I have never seen better than J.C.H. Hunter. Johnny Hunter was a full-back whose middle name should have been Flamboyance. He just set games alight with his running and adventurous attitude. Remember, this was a time when full-backs were not really supposed to attack. Nobody told Johnny. I remember him running back to collect a ball over his own line, sweeping it up, grabbing the post to swing himself back into play and running the length of the field for a try.

He was just as entertaining as a cricketer. At the end of his first season at Fartown he joined Bradley Mills Cricket Club and smashed 178 in his first innings for them, in a first round cup match. Unfortunately he then went and got a duck in the next round. Johnny came down to Birkby Youth Club to help us with our cricket. I don't suppose we could have got luckier.

Huddersfield were always involved in big games in this period. I remember seeing them play in two or three Yorkshire Cup finals and I can remember the 1949 Championship Final at Maine Road as clear as a bell. It was a fantastic affair for us Fartowners and the neutrals, but I suppose Warrington fans were less happy as their team lost 13–12. There were over 75,000 present. It was the biggest crowd ever for a rugby league match in England, apart from for Wembley finals, up to that time. Mind you, the referee failed to turn up and Matt Coates, from Pudsey, one of the touch judges, had to take charge of the match. He became one of the game's top referees and that stroke of luck must have been a big boost to his career.

I also remember two games which were catastrophes for Fartown though. The first was also in 1949. I was sure we were going to get to Wembley, especially when we drew Halifax in the semi-final at Odsal. Halifax were near the bottom of the league and no one in their right mind could see anything but an easy passage for Huddersfield. We should have known better, all 62,000 of us. Halifax played their socks off, stifled Fartown's stars and won 11–10, thanks to a try by Stan Kielty and four goals from Dennis Chalkley. Then in 1950 we met Wigan at Maine Road in the Championship Final for another sure thing. Wigan had eight first teamers missing because they were on their way to Australia and New Zealand with the Lions. Huddersfield amazingly had no players picked for the tour, but were short of Dave Valentine, who must have been injured. Wigan hammered us 20–2 with astonishing ease. It was hardly believable. The crowd for that game was 65,000.

The highlight of this period came in 1953. Huddersfield had a fantastic run in 1952–53, beat Batley in the Yorkshire Cup Final and finished fourth in the league. It was the Challenge Cup though that really brought the thrills. We beat Castleford over two legs in the first round and then knocked Barrow out 21–7 at Fartown. We had nearly 15,000 for the home tie with Castleford and the Barrow game drew 25,608, but those crowds were nothing compared to the third round. Huddersfield won 17–7 at Odsal against Bradford Northern and there were 69,429 counted through the turnstiles.

The semi-final was also played at Odsal, where we beat Wigan 7–0 but the crowd was down to 58,722. I keep mentioning the size of the crowds because I think modern rugby league followers will be amazed at just how popular the game was in those days. I think the crowd for the semi was reduced because it rained torrentially from 9am and as far as I remember never abated until the game ended. I remember some of us made a banner and I had a claret and gold raffia hat, which got so drenched that the dyes ran and my face became a beautiful mixture of red and yellow. So, there's nothing new about face painting.

So Fartown were at Wembley with St Helens as our opponents and I was really excited. I went down by train with my mates Max Ramsden and John Allen. Before the game we went to Trafalgar Square and fed the pigeons and did a bit of sightseeing, taking in the Houses of Parliament and London Bridge. We did not have a lot of time though and the match was obviously the main course. It was my first trip to London and I was aged 17. The atmosphere at Wembley was terrific with 89,588 in attendance. I recall that we stood slightly to the side of the posts but I cannot remember which end.

The critics decided that St Helens were clear favourites. They had finished top of the league, won the Lancashire League and been runners-up in the Lancashire Cup. They only lost two out of 36 games in the league and had also drawn two, one of which was at Fartown. We had been one of the two teams who had beaten them – 17–14 at Knowsley Road. So, what did the critics know? It did not matter what anyone else said or thought, we expected Fartown to win.

Saints certainly intended to win and they didn't seem to care how. They were going for the kill and they didn't play rugby. They got a lot of flak for their strong-arm tactics. The 1953 Challenge Cup final will always be remembered as Peter Ramsden's game. As I mentioned, I played against Peter as a schoolboy and he was a tough opponent. That Cup final day was his 19th birthday and what a day of celebration it proved for him – and us. Talk about youthful exuberance! Peter scored two tries and won the Lance Todd Trophy. Mind you, for one of his tries he was greedy. He had two men outside him and he should have passed. I certainly thought he had blown it but, because he was stocky and unusually strong for a halfback in those days, he could bullock with the best of them and his power took him over.

Saints' unsaintly actions cost them the game that afternoon. It was 5–5 at half-time and then Saints got ahead 8–5 before Billy Banks shot over for a try straight from a scrum and Lionel Cooper kicked the goal. Just a few minutes before Banks scored, Johnny Hunter was laid out by a stiff arm tackle by Saints winger Steve Llewellyn, who was not known for that type of play at all. If anyone was going to be a villain we all thought it would be their hard as nails centre Duggie Greenall. Johnny was spark out and they carted him off on a stretcher and down the tunnel. Ten minutes later Saints got back to 10–10 when George Langfield dropped a goal.

There were only about 10 minutes left when there was a terrific roar as Johnny Hunter, head bandaged, made a dramatic, almost theatrical, return to the field. That just seemed to epitomise him – always the showman. It was like the entry of the gladiator. The noise almost took the roofs off the stands. It certainly lifted our spirits and the team's.

With only four or five minutes to play Ramsden scored the winning try after good work by Dave Valentine and Jim Bowden and Cooper kicked the conversion. 15–10 to Huddersfield and were we happy. The underdogs had won and I just think of the whole day as a magnificent experience. I think we came back on the last train having downed a few beers and arrived home in the early hours of the morning.

A week later we met Saints again in the semi-final of the Championship at Knowsley Road. They just beat us 46–0 and went on to defeat Halifax in the final. But we had won the one that mattered; look at the record books. That's what I always tell the St Helens officials whenever I go to games or functions at Knowsley Road. Of course, Saints have won the Challenge Cup often enough since 1953 and at the time of writing, Fartown have never won it again. That's sport for you.

# 4. Settling down

When I left the RAF I was 20 years old and my attitude to life and the world had obviously been affected by national service. Life in the forces was bound to make people see things differently. Being away from Huddersfield had been a good thing. It broadened my vision and did me a world of good. However, I was still back in Huddersfield at Wheawill and Sudworth, working on accounts and studying by correspondence course. I do not think I could be classed as mercenary, but I was unhappy about what I was earning. I did not think it was fair on my mam and dad that I could not contribute more financially to them. After a couple of years, my thoughts strayed to leaving Wheawill's and the idea that there may be an opening in commerce or business with better prospects. So I started looking for another position. One day I was summoned to see Fred Crosland, one of the partners at Wheawill's. He asked me if I was looking to leave because he had received a letter from B.F. Broadhead, a textile firm in Huddersfield, asking about me. Wheawill's were very co-operative about my moving. They obviously recognised my situation and did not stand in my way.

Franklin Broadhead was the owner of my new place of work and someone who was well-known at the Borough Club. B.F. Broadhead was what was called 'manufacturers without looms'. They dealt primarily in 'out work'. They bought yarn, sent it to be spun and woven at various mills and then arranged for it to be finished at another mill, if the previous one was not set up to do that. Much of our cloth was shipped to Japan or America using letters of credit for payment. I was employed as a cashier. It was better paid than my last job, but I was still basically office-bound dealing with accounts. Occasionally though they did send me out to try to attract business from other mills. That was really production planning, I suppose.

This was, of course, the 1950s and a time when a job was usually for life. Even so, there were some changes taking place, especially in the textile trade. The tycoon Charles Clore was busy targeting the trade as a whole and took over a lot of local firms, one of which was B.F. Broadhead. That meant I moved from Huddersfield town centre to offices down Leeds Road, about a quarter of a mile from Huddersfield Town's ground. The takeover enabled me to have my first dabble with shares as I dealt with them for Mr Broadhead, who also owned William Thompson Fine Clothes, off Leeds Road. We were really in the heart of Huddersfield's industrial and commercial world down there. Learoyd Brothers, one of our main rivals, was very close, next to ICI. We were also agents for Spamount Woollen Company in Castlederg, Northern Ireland, who specialised in good quality Irish tweeds. Brellons, a small concern out at Kirkheaton, was another part of the business. Our operating title as buyers and sellers was Odersfelt Worsteds, Odersfelt, was the ancient name for Huddersfield, and is in the Domesday Book.

I enjoyed my time at Broadhead's which spanned the years 1958 to 1964, but eventually moved to Henry Hamer and Sons at Ravens Ing Mills, Ravensthorpe in Dewsbury, which eventually became William Graham's. In those days Hamer's styled themselves "fancy woollen manufacturers". At least that is what the advert to which I replied said. It asked for "an experienced man to deal with sales correspondence, shipping and dispatching, and also to organise piece progressing. Good salary and own pension scheme for competent man". They appointed me, so I must have passed muster. Heaven knows why I still have the cutting for the job advert. I suppose it is down to my instinct for hoarding things.

By then it was 1964 and I had already had one major and delightful change to my life in the shape of Elizabeth Mary Lumb. I first met Mary at a Saturday night dance at the Regent Ball Room in Fartown in 1959. Coincidentally, that was where I also first encountered Flash Gordon at the pictures, although Mary clearly had a bigger impact on me. In those days dances were where young men met girls. Girls did not go to pubs on their own. In fact, Mary would not even go into a fish and chip shop on her own. The occasion was the annual dance of Pennine Nomads, which sounds pretty mysterious. It wasn't really. Pennine Nomads were the only ladies cricket team in the Huddersfield area and they were based at the quaint Lepton Highlanders. They had a good side and I recall they had some pretty powerfully built girls in their ranks. After a hug from one or two of them, it was a relief to get battered about by a few opposing prop forwards. Mary did not fall into that category at all – she always had a lovely figure – but she fancied herself as a female Freddie Trueman-fast bowler type. I know it sounds corny, but she certainly bowled me over. We hit it off straight away and she was certainly the best thing that ever happened in my life.

Mary was less than a year younger than me and was a French teacher at Sowerby Bridge Grammar School. She came from farming stock, having been born-and-bred at Exley Hall Farm, which adjoins Siddal in Halifax. She was very bright and had been head girl at Princess Mary's Grammar School in Halifax before studying for her degree at Birmingham University and Montpellier.

Her brother John now owns and runs the farm. He is a real character, familiar to all who visit Chevinedge, which, for the uninitiated, is Siddal Rugby League Club's ground. He is the bloke who literally blows his own trumpet, much to the amusement of the crowd. At the beginning of the 20th century Chevinedge was the site of Halifax Zoo. I suppose that a few amateur rugby league teams who have subsequently visited Chevinedge and got a good hiding would have preferred to have encountered some of the wild animals.

It is often said that farmers are staid and stolid. I think that Mary's father, who was also called John, saw me as a townie from Huddersfield and thought Mary could do better. Her mother, Sally, was a lovely, bright woman, who had worked as a maid for Lord Mackintosh before marrying John. She was better disposed towards me, thank goodness.

The day finally came when I decided that I should ask his permission to marry Mary. I thought that was the correct thing to do in those days, which were more innocent than now. Being a man of few words, his response was a simple 'no'. I was quite taken aback, especially as I had given up an afternoon's rugby to see him. What's more, before I broached the subject I had crawled half a mile for him. When I arrived at Exley Hall Farm that Saturday afternoon, the family were in the field at the side of the house thinning out turnips. That field must have been 200 yards long. I, the townie, thought it would be a good ploy to help out. It might put me in Mary's father's good books. After going up and down that turnip field on my hands and knees, I clearly had not impressed Mr Lumb at all.

He did, however, ultimately decide that I was straight and reliable enough to wed his daughter, even though I was a townie. He even came on holiday with us once to North Berwick in Scotland. While we were there we played golf at St Andrews and Mary parred the last hole in front of that most famous of all clubhouses. More surprisingly, I managed to play the round with the same ball, quite a feat for me, especially with all those gorse bushes ready and waiting to gobble up any stray shots.

Mary got on with my parents from the beginning. In fact, she was quick to side with them against me. Mam and dad had been saying they wanted to get a television set, but I had brought up all sorts of objections to the proposal. We didn't need one, we had a wireless, there were better things to do with our time. Really, I was being selfish and irrational because my parents were increasingly tied to the house. Anyway, Mary and they decided that I was not getting my way and when I arrived home one day a television set had usurped the corner where the wireless used to be.

I should have understood that women usually get their way. Mothers and wives are normally the anchor of any family. As a couple Mam and dad were pretty easy going, but I remember one occasion when Mam decided that dad had to do as he was told. She decided he had to mend my bike. I can't remember whether it was the brakes or a puncture, or both. Anyway, he had come home from a visit to the Horse Shoe slightly the worse for wear and she thought he would be better off doing the job without any interference or distractions. So she decided that she and I would be off to the pictures, leaving him at home – locked in.

Mary and I were married on 5 August 1964 and set up our first home at High Bank in Exley, not far from the farm. Actually, the house overlooked the cemetery. We only ever lived in two houses throughout our marriage. Our son Adam was born in 1968, but I will have plenty to say about him later on. I stayed at Hamer's until 1969. By then I had decided that I wanted a change of direction and was determined to set up in business for myself. Mary supported me, as she always was. We both had good jobs, so money was not really an issue, and to tell the truth, I did not really know what business I wanted to get into.

In the end, after looking at various enterprises, we set up a dairy delivery business. I don't suppose I became the fastest milkman in the West (of Yorkshire) but we did make a success of the business, although Mary carried on teaching. The business dovetailed quite well with our association with the farm, which supplied us with eggs and potatoes. I also delivered milk and cream. It was hard work and meant I had to get up at three or four o'clock in the morning – every morning.

To begin with I had a brand new Austin J4 pick-up which was amazingly prone to breakdowns. I decided to go straight to the top with my complaints and wrote to Lord Stokes, the head of British Motors. I got a reply too, but moved on to a Volkswagen, which was more reliable. My correspondence with Lord Stokes became something of a running joke in the family. I suppose that was one of the earliest instances of my predilection for going straight for the top man, when I wanted something. Our plan was to conduct the business for five years – just like one of those Soviet five year plans and that is just about how long it lasted.

By the autumn of 1973 I had had enough of getting up that early in the morning and decided to return to the world of accountancy and textiles. Consequently, I applied for a job as production manager at the Longwood Finishing Company at Parkwood Mills in Longwood, where I stayed for the next few years. In some respects it felt like I had returned to square one. The position at Longwood Finishing was a responsible one. In effect, I was an executive general manager of a workforce of about 100 people. I was responsible for engaging all employees and for subsequent personnel and welfare work, together with production planning, sales and customer liaison and the commercial viability of the company. While I was there I was a founder member and executive of the Milnsbridge Textile Training Group.

The move back into the world of textiles allowed me to operate more normally. I had weekends free again, we had negotiated successfully the period before Adam's entry to school and a regular guaranteed income was essential as Mary was then doing part-time teaching because of our domestic circumstances. Another advantage was that it allowed me to indulge my obsession with rugby league, which had grown even stronger.

Adam was in hospital with a 'hole in the heart' condition when he was aged 10 or 11. I used to ring Eddie Waring regularly, and in one of his commentaries on television, he said 'Best wishes to Adam in Killingbeck Hospital'. I always thought that Eddie had a lot of charisma, and thought he was good for the game, although other people criticised him.

Family memories: From top left, clockwise: Mary with Adam, aged 3 weeks; Maurice with Adam; Mary with Adam around 1 year old; Adam as a toddler.

# 5. Playing for Underbank Rangers

After leaving the RAF I had resumed playing amateur rugby league. I joined Underbank Rangers, one of the most famous of all amateur clubs. I went there because a few of my friends had also decided that was to be their club. From memory, Max Ramsden was the first to go there and Brian Harrison, a centre, who was also employed in textile accountancy, joined the club. We often had tea at our house before going off to training. Mam did the honours before we made the awkward journey from Birkby to Holmfirth on foot and two buses. Another former schoolmate, Geoff Hill, who remains one of my dearest friends, also threw his lot in with Underbank. He ultimately became the club treasurer and public relations officer.

Underbank is a district of Holmfirth, the Pennine town which is the setting for *Last of the Summer Wine*. It is a lovely place and some of my happiest days were spent playing there. I have always loved Holmfirth. The bleak moor land dominates everything. It can be ravishingly beautiful or unbelievably stark, according to weather and season. In winter it could be awful. I remember one game when some kids had managed to build an igloo at one corner of the pitch and there was another occasion when one of our team, a National Service lad on leave from Egypt, had to be carried off suffering from exposure.

Underbank play at a ground called The Cross and there has been a club in Holmfirth for over a century. Harold Wagstaff – 'The Prince of Centres' – is from the town and started his career with Underbank, playing in the first team before he turned 15. He became one of rugby league's iconic figures, captaining Fartown's famous 'Team of all the Talents' in the years straddling The Great War and led Lions tours in 1914 and 1920. He was one of the first inductees into the Rugby League Hall of Fame in 1988.

The club can also boast another Hall of Famer in Neil Fox, rugby league's most prolific points scorer, although Neil did the opposite of Waggie and finished his career playing as an amateur at Underbank after he had turned 40. I am immensely proud that I represented the same club as those two giants of our sport, even if I did not quite measure up to their standards as a player. Of course, I am not old enough to have met Wagstaff, but I have often been in Neil's company. He is a lovely man, still one of my heroes, and is a credit to the game.

David Jeanes, Ian Brooke and Neil Fox while playing for Underbank.

Underbank: 1982 Holliday Cup winners, led by Neil Fox. In the professional game Neil was the world record points scorer, and was player-coach at Underbank. (Both photos courtesy Neil Fox).

In my day, Underbank ran just one open–age side and we played in maroon and amber hoops – a bit like Fartown's claret and gold. Jack Stacey was the driving force at the club. Anyone who met him will remember him; he was a real character. Short, stocky and a former player, he was a plumber and electrician, a good businessman and a local, independent councillor. He later ran a restaurant, Fernleigh, at Holmbridge. Jack did not like losing. If we lost he would give the referee his fee in pennies. Once he was a touch judge in a match I played in. I took a kick at goal and missed by a good five yards. It did not stop Jack from raising his flag for a goal though. He got good support at Underbank from Jack Marsh, who now rests in the nearby cemetery, and Frank Roberts, a good chap, whose daughters used to help out with the refreshments.

To say things were a bit primitive in my playing days would be an understatement. The pitch sloped in every direction and always will. Undulating would be a very fair description. However, it did give us a definite playing advantage. I was a reasonable punter of the ball, but my 40 yard kicks became 70 yarders when the wind blew down field.

To get to the pitch from the dressing-rooms – I use the term loosely – we had to go from the main road through a farmyard – cow dung, pong and all. We got used to it, but visiting sides must have wondered what they had let themselves in for. The foot-and-mouth disaster a few years back caused all sorts of problems for the farm and the club. Rangers had to play all their games away from home and came close to folding. Thankfully, they clung on. Something you can count on with rugby league folk is their resilience in the face of long odds.

I remember playing at Underbank as a schoolboy. An old house served as the dressing rooms. It was all stone floors and the showers were a sight to behold. The shower heads were four Heinz beans tins, punctured where the water flew out. They were still there when I played as an amateur, although maybe they were different tins by then. Still, we were lucky to have showers at all in those prehistoric times. It was about half a mile from the dressing rooms to the playing field. We would point out where the pitch was to our opponents, who would proceed through the farmyard and its delights and trudge up the hill, often in freezing conditions. We would wait and then go up in a couple of cars. We weren't daft. I never did discover whether Jack Stacey was responsible for the plumbing of our showers.

After the match we would all retire to the Shoulder of Mutton in Holmfirth for refreshments. The pub is often seen on *Last of the Summer Wine*.

While I was at Underbank a proper clubhouse was built. Many of the lads were tradesmen and brought their professional skills to the project. Even though I was just an office walla, I did my share of the labouring, pushing countless wheelbarrows full of sand and building materials for the skilled workers.

I played at Underbank between 1955 and 1963, but spent some periods playing for Crosland Moor, which later became Moldgreen ARL Club. Underbank had a pretty good side when I arrived at The Cross with a couple of good half-backs in Charlesworth and Dickinson. I eventually got in the team, mostly at scrum-half, although I occasionally played centre or stand-off. I had become player-coach and captain by the time I hanged up my boots. We won the Holiday Cup and the Huddersfield & District Championship in my time at the club. For a while we competed in a joint Huddersfield and Halifax league.

One year we got to the semi-final of the Yorkshire Cup only to be robbed of a place in the final when Eric Clay, the great test match referee, denied us a crucial try for a forward pass. I suppose he could have been right, although none of us thought so at the time.

I was fortunate not to have suffered too many injuries as an amateur rugby league player, although I did have a penchant for breaking my collar-bone. The second time I broke it, I did not go to hospital until the Sunday following the game. Young and daft, I thought it more important not to miss the Saturday night dance.

I also remember a painful trip to Hull, while I was at Moldgreen. We had gone to play in a friendly at a club, details of which I can longer remember, except that their dressing rooms were a railway carriage on the bottom side of the playing field. What I do remember is that, as an exceptional treat, we had arranged to have a slap-up meal of ham, bacon and eggs after the match. That was a big deal in those days and I was really looking forward to it. Anyway, during the game a Hull player made a slashing break and I chased after him. As I dived to make the tackle, his heel came up and cracked me hard on the jaw. One of my teeth flew out and landed in my hand. It was amazing, but bloody painful. My jaw was so tender that I was unable to eat the slap-up meal. Was I upset!

The dentist was closed on the Sunday and when I saw him on the Monday, he said he could not do anything as my jaw might be broken. He told me to go away for a week and see if the swelling subsided. I had to take the week off work because it was so painful. He sorted my tooth out the following Friday. I am pleased to say I still have all my own teeth and have never had a filling, despite my very sweet tooth.

A game I played for Underbank against Moldgreen brings back memories and says something about my temperament. I was playing scrum-half and we won a scrum. There appeared to be no option to run or pass though, so I decided just to subside against the scrummage before playing the ball. As I lapsed into an almost sitting-like position the Moldgreen scrum-half, Colin Ackroyd, a tough customer who had been a pro at Batley, belted me hard across the nose. Our stand-off Keith Dyson, a good soccer player and cricketer, rushed in to exact retribution on Colin. Somehow, through the fuzz of blood and despite my undignified position on the ground, I managed to restrain Keith, while shouting "No! We have a cup-tie next week!" I think that demonstrated my ability to absorb punishment, long fuse and ability to look to the future, despite what some other people might think. What's a bloody nose worth?

In the old days amateur rugby league could be a brutal affair with frequent resort to fisticuffs. Jack McNamara, that fine journalist with the *Manchester Evening News*, once described pre-BARLA amateur rugby league as tribal warfare and he was not wrong. I particularly remember a game against Ravensthorpe All Blacks. It was a morning game and must have been either at Easter or in May, because the team had arranged to go on an outing to Manchester races in the afternoon. The All Blacks had a lot of hard-bitten former pros and the odd homicidal maniac in their ranks, or at least that's how it appeared to teams playing against them. One, David Peace, had played for Doncaster and Blackpool Borough. He was a hard man and no mistake.

At some point in the game he glowered at me and said "I'll get you". God knows what I was supposed to have done. I never looked for trouble, so I just smiled at him and went about my business. Later on I got tackled and David came in as third man with malevolent intent. Fortunately, the second tackler had his elbow across my face as we hit the ground. David's boot smashed into the elbow and the poor second tackler was carted off.

37

I realised now that David Peace had meant what he said. Later on I caught him with a perfectly judged, legal crash tackle. I was a bit of a specialist in that art, despite usually being the smallest man on the pitch. I had always been capable of tackling the biggest of opponents since I played the game as a child. It was an ability in which I took pride. Anyway, the tackle must have really taken the wind out of David, who left the field, much to my relief. However, to my horror, with about eight minutes left, he returned to the field. I can tell you that from that point, wherever the play went, I went the other way; otherwise I know I would never have got to those races at Manchester.

In those days there was an annual end of season competition staged at Rastrick for pub teams. The sides were composed of new players and established amateur players. Additionally, a few professionals were allowed to play. I remember Peter Ramsden, Frank Dyson and Peter Henderson were some of the Fartowners who took part. I used to enter a team called the Barbarians and after my close encounter with David Peace, I made sure that the first person I invited to play for the side was that man. We needed a hard man, but as far as I was concerned the main priority was that he was not in any of the opposing teams. What is that about discretion being the better part of valour? Frank Dyson certainly subscribed to that. Frank, a Great Britain full-back, was a very hard player, but not dirty. He certainly would not shirk anything as a professional. The Barbarians came up against the side Frank was representing and we were attacking downhill. We put up a long, high ball which came down in the middle of Frank's '25'. It bobbled about and there was no doubt that Frank could easily have fallen on it, but he looked over his shoulder, spotted David Peace bearing down on him like the clap of doom and simply hoofed the ball out of play. He told me there was no way he was going down on that ball with Peace coming down on him. He wasn't even getting paid. I always thought that was very wise of Frank.

I understand that David is still alive – and I hesitate to say kicking – and I want to assure him that I have no intention of making a comeback. I have seen him occasionally in the street or at a match.

# 6. Refereeing

I was 28 when I decided to give up playing. I had begun to get the urge to take up refereeing. While I had been lucky with injuries, my decision to forsake playing for reffing was partly due to a shoulder problem I developed. As I said, I never had problems with tackling, but one day I carried the ball into a tackle and positioned myself wrongly. Instead of riding with the first tackler, I braced myself for the second man and took his momentum full on the shoulder. The injury plagued me for about half the season, but I played through it. You got no sympathy for minor injuries in amateur rugby league. I finally realised that there was something really wrong when I played tennis with Mary in Scarborough and found that I could not even throw the balls up high enough to serve. In rugby league, I did not exactly go out at the top.

I enjoyed my time as a referee. Refereeing means being involved all the game. You are on your own, even though you might have touch-judges. I have never minded taking criticism, so name calling and irate supporters did not bother me. Mary and my father were less happy about the abuse, but I was impervious to it. I always made a point of going to the after match functions at the local pub or at one of that rare breed, the clubhouse. I considered it would have been cowardice not to have done so and, anyway, there was never any real bother once the game was over. I realise that some people think there is no such thing as a good referee, but I will always defend officials. Contrary to what the referee baiters believe, referees never start brawls, never throw punches, never perpetrate stiff-arm tackles. It is the players who do that.

Whatever anyone thinks of referees, it is greatly to the game's credit that usually everyone accepts their decisions. The discipline in rugby league and the respect for referees from the players is a shining example to the rest of sports. Often behaviour in top level soccer shows just how blessed rugby league is in that respect. The lack of sportsmanship and excess of gamesmanship are appalling and there was a continual striving to cheat on the part of players, whose respect for the referees was abysmally low. No rugby league, or rugby union, referee would ever expect to be subjected to the hassle, intimidation and outright dissent directed at those soccer referees and if, by some great misfortune, they ever were, the rugby authorities would throw the book at the miscreants. Diving and rolling about pretending to be hurt might be acceptable in football but, thank God, rugby players are not like that.

It was Bill Fallowfield, the Rugby Football League secretary, who ran the courses for referees when I took up the whistle. Bill was always very supportive of the referees. However, I am glad he did not see one of my first games, which was Underbank versus Moldgreen. Obviously, the fact that I knew most of the players was going to be either a blessing or a curse. My intention was to be strictly neutral. However, old habits die hard. A scrum went down early in the game and the Moldgreen scrum-half – I think it might have been Colin Ackroyd – piped up, "Whose ball is it, sir?" Straight away I replied, "Ours". Colin's retort was short and sweet – "We're no effing chance today."

I belonged to the Huddersfield & District Rugby League Referees Society and was made very welcome from the start. I got a lot of help from Clarrie Sutcliffe, a little red-haired chap, who ran the line for the deciding World Cup match between Britain and Australia at Odsal in 1960. Other stalwarts I remember were Ian Meskimmon from Brighouse, who was the society's secretary, Jeff Preston, Mick Beaumont, who had been a team-mate at Moldgreen, and John O'Connor, who succeeded Ian as secretary. The society used to meet at The Friendly and Trades Club on Northumberland Street, where they had very positive meetings and lively debates about interpretations of the game's laws. Referees from Dewsbury, Oldham and Rochdale, among other places, frequently attended our meetings and the great Billy Thompson still turned up even after he had become one of the game's very top whistlers. He was a shining example to us all.

Refereeing was not very glamorous at my level. I used to carry a little brown case with all my gear in it, and most importantly an extra shirt in case of a colour clash. The remuneration was seven and sixpence (37½p) for under-17s games, 10 shillings (50p) for under-19s and 15 shillings (75p) for open age matches. Obviously, we did not do it for the money. Ever the accountant though, all my fees went straight into savings stamps. My refereeing career lasted for around a decade, from 1963 to 1973, although the old RFL *Official Guides* had me on their list of active officials as late as 1978–79.

One of my first major appointments was as touch-judge for a Yorkshire versus Lancashire under-17s match at Keighley. I recall that

David Ward, later a captain of Great Britain, signed for Leeds straight after the game. I also remember refereeing a Lancashire versus Yorkshire Youth match at Blackbrook. By then I had retired from refereeing and was employed at BARLA. The designated referee failed to turn up, so I had to take his place. No one had a whistle so I had to referee by voice, which might have been a first. I remember having to smile as Alex Murphy – probably on a scouting mission – barracked me unmercifully from the touchline throughout the game. At least it proved to some doubters that BARLA employees were adaptable characters.

I also was in charge of a Cumberland versus Lancashire Open Age match, which was slightly embarrassing for me because by then I was a BARLA administrator and some people thought that might compromise me in some way. It was not as controversial though as my refereeing appointment for the game against the Australian Combined High Schools at Fartown in 1972.

Politics reared its ugly head when I was suddenly pulled out of the appointment and replaced by Billy Thompson. John O'Connor tried to get the decision reversed and I had the full support of the Referees Society, but Bill Fallowfield and the RFL were determined to have their way. That was the first time I ever suffered punishment for my 'political' views. I know that the decision was retribution for being a leader in the breakaway BARLA movement, which was then in its infancy. I would have loved to have been on the same pitch as that outstanding Australian Schools team, which swept aside all opposition – they played 12, won 12 and scored 402 points while conceding just 17, including a solitary try. There were some real stars in the making among those young Australians, such as Royce Ayliffe, who was the captain, Les Boyd, Ian Schubert and Craig Young, who all went on to represent Australia at test level.

Progressing up the refereeing ladder I officiated at many Yorkshire Senior Competition matches which were the 'A' team (reserve) fixtures for the professional clubs, and I was touch-judge for first team matches at professional level. The biggest game I participated in was the Wakefield Trinity versus New Zealanders fixture in 1971, when I ran the line.

Anyone who has been involved in refereeing rugby league will have had hairy or amusing experiences and I have probably forgotten more than I can remember. Some stick in the mind, however.

Maurice keeping a careful watch as the touch judge when Wakefield Trinity play the Kiwis in 1971.

There was one occasion when I was refereeing a youth game between Flockton and St Mary's, a Halifax side, at Flockton Working Men's Club. Oddly enough, the field was right next door to my uncle's house. St Mary's, who also ran a boxing club, had a huge lad in their team, who seemed to be a giant surrounded by dwarves. His name was Richard Dunn, who went on to fight Muhammad Ali for the World Heavyweight Championship. Things got a bit aerated and Richard threw a real haymaker at an opponent, but failed to connect. I sent him off and he objected: "But I missed!" I replied, "Well, it's not my fault that you missed. If you had hit him you would have put him into orbit." He gave me a false name, saying he was called Bacon. Well, he had had his chips now. I met Richard at Sheffield when Clinton Woods won a World title. He remembered the incident, but thankfully does not hold it against me. Anyone who goes to rugby league at Odsal will notice the Richard Dunn Centre on the opposite side of the road, even if they are not old enough to remember the man after whom it is named.

The Boulevard in Hull is a memorable venue for any referee or touch-judge. It is certainly not a place for faint-hearts because the crowd can be distinctly intimidating. I never really had any bother there though. I do remember an 'A' Team game against Dewsbury, when I was perhaps a bit naïve. A scrum was formed and some extremely foul language emanated from it. I roared, "Cut that language out. There's ladies present." A gnarled hooker, bearing the scars of his trade – a broken nose and cauliflower ears – looked up and smiled before he told me "There's no ladies at The Boulevard, Sir."

Still, it could have been much worse. I do not know whether the tale is true or not but I have often heard about one particular Hull versus Hull KR derby. It was Boxing Day, the season of goodwill, when such matches used to be staged. There was an almighty punch-up and everybody joined in except the Hull full-back, who the referee sent off when everything settled down. "What have you done that for?" asked the full-back, to which the referee replied, "For cowardice". Depending on who is telling the tale, that referee could be Eric Clay, Billy Thompson or Fred Lindop, or anyone else for that matter.

There is no doubt in my mind that Clay, Thompson and Lindop were the best referees I have seen. I thought Clay was brilliant and I got to know him quite well. His nickname of 'Sergeant Major' was very apt. He refereed with a rod of iron and his stentorian voice boomed across the field. Like all great referees, he had that air of confidence and that ability to appear as if he was right, even if he was not.

Billy Thompson, who became a successful after dinner speaker, was quick, decisive, confident and always wanted to get on with the game. Even if he gave a wrong decision, 90 percent of the crowd would not realise it and even the most hard done to players could be convinced they were in the wrong. Billy must have been exceptional because the Australians appointed him as referee to the first State of Origin match.

Fred Lindop must have been exceptional too because he refereed an Ashes series in 1967 when he was aged 29 and continued to referee in the Pennine League well into his sixties. He was appointed to the RFL Roll of Honour in 2009. Fred was always supremely fit, mobile and oozed self-confidence. Off the field he was something of an introvert, a bit insular, but I got on well with him and he would often make a point of sitting with me at various functions. He did a lot of junior coaching for his local side at Eastmoor in Wakefield and put loads of work in at Sheffield University. He was a big driving force in university rugby league and was prepared to go anywhere to help rugby league at grassroots level. That is one of the things which always struck me about both Billy and Fred – their commitment to the amateur side of the game. Billy would be quite willing to referee a junior game in the morning before taking a big professional appointment in the afternoon or evening. I always found both very approachable.

Billy had an unusual experience while fulfilling a BARLA appointment in France. Our District League champions, Hull had the reward of playing a game in Perpignan and Billy was given the appointment. Hull had some great players such as Bob Colgrave and Steve Critchenson – legends in the amateur game. The French pulled a bit of a stroke by fielding the Catalans team – all top class players – but at half-time Hull were leading. It was then that Billy got a real shock. The French substituted him with one of their own officials and Hull eventually lost.

If that was not bad enough, fog and bad weather conspired to prevent Billy and the Hull lads from leaving Perpignan for several days because planes were grounded. Billy was not too pleased and still brings the subject up. He will say to me: "You know, Maurice, BARLA still owes me money for those five days in Perpignan. I never got paid." My response is always: "Come on, Billy, you only did half a game, so you owe BARLA half your fee and, don't forget, you got a free holiday." I think I slipped him a fiver out my own pocket.

One of the benefits of having the dairy business had been the freedom to referee university rugby league matches on Wednesday afternoons. It gave me a great deal of pleasure and satisfaction to be able to play a part in helping university rugby league in its infancy. I loved taking games at establishments like Leeds University and De La Salle College. A lot of the students came from rugby union backgrounds and wore shorts with pockets. I used to tell them "You'll not have time to put your hands in those pockets playing this game."

Refereeing kept me fit and I enjoyed the social side; mixing with the players and people involved in the sport. I always found it wonderful how players respected the referee. If a player threw the ball away in a fit of pique, frustration or anger, I would tell him to fetch it and he would meekly do as he was told, bring the ball back and present it to me like the head of John the Baptist. It did not matter whether he was the biggest, ugliest, hardest beggar on the planet; he knew that he had to respect the referee. As players we were always taught not to argue with the referee and to address him as "Sir". Without that respect for the officials, rugby league would be much the poorer. In fact it would probably be unmanageable. Players give and take punishment in true gladiatorial style, get on with the game, and have a pint afterwards.

44

# 7. The birth of BARLA

In 1972 I was president of the Huddersfield Referees Society. I was not happy about the state of rugby league in general, but particularly at amateur level. Despite the fact that amateur clubs had begun to spring up in the Midlands and the south of England, as well as in the universities, the game in its heartlands appeared to be dying on its feet. Youth rugby had virtually collapsed and Lancashire could not even raise a side for the county championship. One reason was the insistence of professional clubs on forming supporters' teams, which was counter-productive and selfish. The supporters' teams were for junior players. The good players would gravitate to the professional clubs, which could weaken the local amateur sides, and even lead to their collapse.

The district leagues appeared to be in terminal decline. I remember often going to referee games only to find that one of the teams had not been able to raise 13 players and had to call off the game. It was ruining my weekends. Hardly any amateur clubs ran more than one side and by the time the RFL *Official Guide* came out at the beginning of the season some of the clubs listed no longer even operated. It was completely hit-and-miss as far as fulfilling fixtures was concerned. Even worse was the realisation that no one at the RFL seemed to care.

Before the foundation of BARLA, the amateur game was governed by the RFL. The amateurs had no representation on the Rugby League Council. There were three County Amateur Commissions, Cumberland, Lancashire and Yorkshire, which were supposed to administer the game. Each had a five-man committee and the leaders of each committee, the honorary secretaries (or commissioners), who received an honorarium from the RFL, were unelected. In essence Bill Fallowfield, the RFL secretary, appointed them annually. Bill, to all intents and purposes a dictator, presided over what was a shambles as far as the amateurs were concerned. Although I ended up on a collision course with him in the short term, we got along well in the aftermath and became good friends.

Really, all the RFL did for the amateur game was organise one open age international and one junior (under-19s) international against France each season, alternately in England and France. The English Schools Rugby League did a pretty good job, but once boys left school there was virtually no provision for them to continue to play the game. Many simply went to play rugby union, which provided good facilities and continuous opportunities to play at different age groups. These players were lost to rugby league. In fact, I had been worried for quite a while about the lack of provision and opportunities for boys and youths. I regarded the promotion of the game at those levels as vital for the future of the sport. Locally, I thought that we needed to get a Youth League going in Huddersfield or the game would wither away. I made approaches to Hubert Lockwood, one of the great men of rugby league, who had been a fantastic full-back with Huddersfield and Halifax. Hubert was club chairman at Fartown and had just finished his stint as chairman of the Rugby League Council, the game's governing body. I had suggested to him that the RFL should promote a schoolboy curtain-raiser to the Challenge Cup final at Wembley and he supported the concept. Ironically, the English Schools Rugby League turned the idea down because they felt that the Wembley pitch would be too big for schoolboys. In fact, the under-11 match before the final has been a great success and part of a vibrant and growing schools competition.

In the meantime, there was an even more pressing problem to resolve – the governance of the amateur rugby league game, perhaps its very existence. I don't know whether there is something in the water around Huddersfield which inoculates some of us with the rugby league bug, but I sometimes think there must be. Rugby league was born in Huddersfield in 1895, as I constantly remind folk. It was also in Huddersfield that amateur rugby league was resurrected three-quarters of a century later. While I recognise that it was just a coincidence, it is a happy coincidence for a Huddersfield lad like me. What was really fortunate was the presence of two rugby league fanatics, Tom Keaveney and Jack Clayton, in the same place at the same time. Tom Keaveney was the real driving force in the movement which gave birth to the British Amateur Rugby League Association (BARLA).

Tom was secretary of the St Joseph's ARLC and also secretary of the Huddersfield District Rugby League. He had attained that position after effectively engineering a coup within the society. Jack Clayton became the chairman. I was involved as the representative of the Referees' Society and had a place on the committee. Tom was a clerk with the Yorkshire Electricity Board and worked in offices at Birchencliffe, where I would go to see him at lunch time when matters needed to be discussed. We were about the same age. As a young man Tom had been studying to become a Roman Catholic priest, but contracted muscular dystrophy and his hopes of the priesthood were dashed. His condition meant he had to use a wheelchair and far from inhibiting him, it seemed to galvanise him. I do not think I have ever met a stronger-willed man than Tom Keaveney. He had so much strength of character. In some sense he could be described as ruthless and people definitely deferred to him. He usually got his own way and he was always on the phone.

I heard people say that Tom would not live to see 40, but he did and his fight to establish BARLA appeared to me to be a big factor in keeping him going and giving him the ability to prioritise matters properly. If I thought he was a man-and-a-half, Mary was in total admiration of him. She always said: "Tom is worth any 20 of the rest of them," and she meant it. Tom drove his own car but I remember one occasion when Bob Beal, who later became chairman of BARLA, was absolutely terrified when travelling with him, because Moira, Tom's wife, helped him to turn difficult corners by assisting him with the steering wheel. We all survived though. Both Tom and Bob were deservedly honoured by the Queen for their services to amateur rugby league. Tom received the MBE in 1978 and Bob was awarded the OBE six years later.

Jack Clayton made an excellent chairman. He was an education welfare officer, what we used to call the 'board man' – he had that in common with another wonderful rugby league character, Trevor Foster, the great Welsh forward, who served Bradford Northern and Bradford Bulls so loyally for over 60 years. Jack was an absolute whiz when it came to local government affairs. He sat on lots of committees, was a great front man and had an air of authority – some people might have thought of it as pompous. For BARLA he was a sort of elder statesman. Apart from being a good chairman, he was a keen crown green bowler and loved ballroom dancing.

Tom, Jack and I formed a sort of triumvirate in Huddersfield amateur rugby league affairs, but Tom was the prime mover. It was Tom who decided it was time to do something for the amateur game in the widest sense. He wrote to all the district leagues and invited them to a meeting at Greenside Working Men's Club on 4 March 1973.

The meeting duly took place and in its own way was as significant as that famous 1895 meeting at the George Hotel. The place was packed with representatives from all over rugby league land and there was unanimity that there should be a breakaway from the RFL. I recall the meeting as entirely positive and there was a feeling of euphoria at what we had done. Jack was elected chairman of the newly formed committee, Tom was secretary and I was assistant secretary and PRO.

I realised, along with many others, that the meeting at the Greenside Working Men's Club in Moldgreen might well prove to be of historic importance, but amateur rugby league was not a priority as far as the national newspapers were concerned. The following morning Jack Bentley's very short rugby league column in the *Daily Express* was headlined "Referee chinned". Terry Keane, an official from Oldham, had been hit by a spectator at the close of the Bradford Northern versus Wigan Challenge Cup quarter-final at Odsal. Bradford had caused a surprise by winning 11–7 before a crowd of 23,525; the club's biggest for seven years, according to Bentley. It was certainly a bigger gathering than had attended at Greenside, but Bentley still had space to write "Amateur rugby league formed its own controlling body at Huddersfield yesterday. Representatives of more than 200 clubs in the North, Midlands, Southern Counties and universities voted to form the British Amateur Rugby League Association. Said Mr Jack Clayton of Huddersfield, chairman of the new body's working party: 'With so many problems in the professional game the Rugby League Council does not have the time to look after the amateurs'."

That was a nice piece of diplomatic understatement. The announcement of the formation of BARLA was, of course, very exciting for us activists, but we had triggered a war with the RFL. Bill Fallowfield was quick to attack us. He instructed the professional clubs not to put their facilities and grounds at our disposal, had the RFL declare it would no longer support any amateur club which decided to join our new organisation and even issued a libel writ against the *Hull Daily Mail*, which had the temerity to publish some letters offering support and goodwill towards BARLA.

At a Council meeting in April, 1973 the RFL voted 29–1 not to recognise BARLA and branded us as "a rebel group". The only vote in our favour was by Tom Mitchell, the Workington Town representative on the Council. Needless to say, BARLA was not allowed to have even an observer present. The RFL issued a circular saying that BARLA was unconstitutional and that any club, official or player connected with it would be barred from receiving any benefit from the RFL or its clubs. Tom Keaveney was reported as saying "Mr Fallowfield's circular virtually amounted to blackmail if we did not toe his line." With friends like the RFL and enemies like the RFU, things did not look too bright.

Crucially, The Sports Council had been founded in 1972 and we knew that we had to get it on our side in the struggles that lay ahead. A government organisation, its brief was to promote amateur sport. Moreover, it was responsible for providing public funding to suitable sporting bodies. I, for one, thought that amateur rugby league was a prime candidate for such financial support, particularly as I understood that ballroom dancing, or maybe it was folk-dancing, had recently received a grant of £18,000. If we did not qualify, who did?

Through this early period there were more meetings at Greenside WMC and later at the Irish League Club in Huddersfield. We had a working executive committee of seven or eight people, besides Tom, Jack and me. Meetings were held monthly, but in between them there was much to do and organise. It took up a lot of time and I was once again grateful to have such a supportive wife as Mary.

What was blindingly obvious was that we needed to develop the game and to do that we needed professional people to run the organisation. That was why it was so essential to get access to the Sports Council's funding. At first I thought we needed a national coach, but I was totally wrong on that score. The Sports Council told us in no uncertain terms that the administration came first. Coaches were no use if no one organised the actual games. We had to demonstrate our own stability and progress and draw up sensible development plans. Moreover, there would not be any funding forthcoming until we proved our financial viability. Like any other amateur sporting organisation, our member leagues, clubs and players would have to pay for the privilege of playing their chosen sport.

When BARLA was formed I was still a production manager at Ravensthorpe, Tom Keaveney was at the Yorkshire Electricity Board and Jack Clayton was a welfare officer. I spent a lot of time chasing around with Tom, was still refereeing and was chairman of the Huddersfield Referees Society, which had some pretty good members.

BARLA Officers: Clockwise from top left: Bob Beal (vice-chairman), Jack Clayton (chairman), Maurice Oldroyd (national administrator) and Tom Keaveney MBE (Secretary).

Maurice with Jack Clayton, BALRA chairman, under the BARLA umbrella.

A BARLA Management Committee: Back row: J. Tonge, G. Owen, D. Scott, J. McDowall, E. Hanson; front: H. Swift, Maurice, J. Clayton, T. Keaveney, R. Beal.

The BARLA officials who were awarded the Silver Jubilee Medal in 1977:
Standing (from left);
J.A. Clayton and E. Hanson;
Sitting:
E. Houghton, R.A. Beal and T.E. Beautiman.

BARLA was an organisation formed by amateurs, for amateurs and run by amateurs. In other words we had no paid officers. Nor did we have an office. The whole thing was run from Tom's house and Jack's office at Huddersfield Corporation. It was clear from day one that the volume of work meant that we needed a professional officer. So we put our case to the Sports Council and they agreed that we could have one full-time officer and a back-up typist/secretary.

That full-time officer post really appealed to me. Of course, the job had to be advertised and there were other applicants apart from me. This was not until August 1976, three years after the birth of BARLA, I should say. The interviews were conducted by a Sports Council representative, Jack Clayton and Tom Mitchell. I remember there was a retired naval officer up for the post, who seemed to think that a lot of power would come with the position. I think I had a more realistic view of what it would involve. I thought that the job was made to measure for me. I knew the grassroots and the schools set-up; had played the game and refereed it and I also had a background in accounts and administration. In other words, I felt qualified and although it would be a big gamble, Mary backed me.

Tom Mitchell and Bob Beal also backed me. Tom told the other members of the interviewing committee that if they really wanted me, they should choose me, because if they picked someone else they would be making a mistake. I should say that I was not fed up with my day job and would have probably bumbled along in it, if I had not been appointed to the BARLA post. The job title was national administrator.

In a sense BARLA was lucky with its timing. Bill Fallowfield retired from the RFL not long after the birth of the association. There were high levels of dissatisfaction with Bill throughout the game. He was a total dictator and basically got away with that style of behaviour until he left. I remember a meeting one dark dismal November day, which was going nowhere. He stood up, walked over to the light switch and said "Let's throw some light on this". He was very arrogant and dismissive of people. He was more or less saying "I'll have to do it myself." His departure removed one big impediment to progress. I remember one official saying after a RL council meeting "At least Bill treats us all the same – like shit."

Ultimately, though, we did get on – but not until after Bill stepped down. Actually, even the RFL only had a handful of full-time workers and at one point we did some of their typing to help out, which must have indicated things were improving. A few years after BARLA was formed, Bill and I were both at an International Board meeting in Australia and he had a heart attack. I didn't cause it, but Bill's attitude towards the amateurs in those early days could have caused some of us to have heart problems. He was really resistant to our cause.

I am a bit of a hoarder. In fact since Mary died in 2001, I have probably got worse. However, saving old documents, reports, letters and publications is very useful when it comes to writing about history and I have got plenty of material to jog my memory. Bill Fallowfield showed his teeth in a circular he sent out on 30 March, 1973. It did not have a heading, just a reference number: RFL/141/73. It was very hostile to BARLA, and is reproduced as Appendix 1 in this book, along with Tom Keaveney's reply.

Bill distributed his circular to the "District Leagues, Amateur Clubs, the Rugby League Council (for information) and the Sports Council". It was full of his typical bluster and intimidatory tactics and some of it was just not true. Happily, the founding fathers of BARLA were not intimidated or deceived. Our acting secretary, Tom Keaveney responded devastatingly with a circular of BARLA's own on 4 April, 1973. It was distributed to "All English District Leagues, all English amateur clubs, all professional clubs, the Rugby Football League and the Sports Council". Tom was clearly in bullish mood, as we all were, and furious with Fallowfield's misrepresentations.

Bill Fallowfield continued to be obstructive to BARLA, refused to arrange a meeting with us and came up with the idea of forming a National Amateur League. In one of his circulars he wrote, "Eventually if the National League comes into being it may be possible to form two, three or even more divisions. There is no doubt that the old District League system of operating amateur Rugby League Football is now completely out of date. The fact that many District Leagues operate no competitions but have to send their teams as guests into other areas supports this view".

Talk about condemning yourself from your own mouth – at least he was at last acknowledging something needed to be done about amateur rugby league. His National Amateur League proposal was aimed at an elite section of amateur clubs, who would have their own secretary and would be financed by the RFL. Tom Keaveney recognised the flaw and wrote: "So yet again the lesser mortals in the amateur game will be completely ignored." Bill's proposals never addressed the major problems.

BARLA had already drawn up a forward plan. Tom wrote on 28 June 1973: "The top priority, as stated in our development plan is, logically, to plan for the future, and this means capturing 15 to 18-year-old youths now and so ensuring a reservoir of talent for tomorrow. The success of all good building and healthy growth is, as always, from the bottom and not from the top, a point that seems to be completely lost in [Bill Fallowfield's] latest circular".

It was the creation of our forward plan that pulled us all together in the early days of BARLA. Our emphasis was on youth rugby, domestic expansion and international expansion. Above all our big thrust was toward youth football, which became a huge success. That was the passport to public money, a point which cannot be overemphasized, and it gave us a significant track record. The RFL had simply not looked after youth rugby, which had declined almost catastrophically. There had been virtually no youth development.

Looking back, things moved quickly although it might not have seemed quick enough at the time. Bill Fallowfield must have known that we were not going to cave in but neither was he and it was another eight months before peace began to break out. Brian Smith wrote in the Bradford Saturday night's pink *Yorkshire Sports* of 23 February 1974: "It hasn't been all gloom this week for the news that BARLA and the Rugby League Council have settled their differences could be a great boon for the game. BARLA have had overwhelming support from the amateur leagues in their aim to be allowed to run the amateur game as an independent organisation and, more and more, rugby league as a whole needs a thriving amateur set-up if the game as a whole is to survive. The BARLA officials reflect the sort of faith in the future which the game sadly needs from more professional clubs who are content to sit back and reckon the world owes them a living".

A meeting of the Amateur Working Party took place at Chapeltown Road a fortnight later, on Saturday 9 March 1974. This group made some momentous decisions on that Saturday morning in Leeds. I have a copy of the minutes. Ronnie Simpson of Castleford chaired the meeting and the others present were Brian Snape (Salford), M.J. Lumb, J. Elliott, J. Holmes, L. Hardy, Tom Keaveney, D. Scott, Bob Beal, K.

Humphries, Harold Swift and me. It helped that Bill Fallowfield was not present. The main task was to deal with the proposed constitution of "an Amateur Rugby League Council". The minutes show that "the BARLA representatives stated that BARLA had virtually done this. BARLA was seeking autonomy on the basis of their five-year development plan. It was their intention to have close liaison with the Rugby League Council and they did not wish to isolate the amateurs entirely. [However] they wished to have complete autonomy for the amateurs."

The BARLA representatives listed four main reasons for seeking autonomy:

a) The amateurs should be entirely separate from the professionals, as was the case with the English Schools RL.

b) Expansion would be easier if they were not controlled by the professional game.

c) Financial assistance towards administration, development and national coaches could be obtained from the Sports Council.

d) Development on a national scale would be easier if the rugby union barrier could be removed.

Wonderfully, the meeting ended in complete agreement that there should be "an autonomous amateur organisation" and the following proposals were carried unanimously:

1) "That this working party recommend to the Rugby League Council that an autonomous body be set up to be responsible for the development and administration of Amateur Rugby League".

2) "That the working party can see no reason why this new association should not be called The British Amateur Rugby League Association".

3) "That the present administration of the British Amateur Rugby League Association will continue as at present and a Rugby League Liaison committee will be set up to consist of equal representation from the amateurs and the professionals to meet at least twice a year".

BARLA's fight for recognition had been won. It was a lovely feeling but we had plenty of work ahead of us.

By July 1974 Bill Fallowfield had retired and was replaced by David Oxley. Bill and I had one thing in common. We were both former RAF men. He was a Flight Lieutenant, a Cambridge graduate and an England Services rugby union international forward. I only got as far as being an SAC (Senior Aircraftsman) and scrum-half for Underbank. I suppose they are right when they say it takes all sorts. As I said, Bill and I later became better disposed towards each other. Bill had been Secretary of the International Board (IB) since its inception and even after he retired as secretary of the RFL he remained secretary of the IB. We consequently ran into each other all over the world as members of the IB.

Although David Oxley was an Oxford graduate, he was a completely different kettle of fish to Bill Fallowfield. David was a superb ambassador for the game and it was a good day for our sport and for BARLA's future relations with the RFL when they appointed him.

Of course, BARLA was fortunate in having men of integrity and good standing in its ranks in those early days. One of the things I thought essential was a body of top class vice-presidents and, backed by Tom Keaveney and Jack Clayton, I picked a first class team. By 1976 our vice-presidents were Jack Clayton, David Oxley, Ronnie Simpson, Sumner Baxendale, Brian Snape, Fred Haworth, Eddie Waring and Kevin Humphreys (Australia). Our patron was Tom Mitchell and our president was Harry Womersley. Our executive committee members were all top men from their regions: Edgar Hanson, Stuart McDonough, Geoff Owen, Jim Rogerson, Tom Barlow and Harold Swift; while our chairman was Bob Beal and our vice-chairman was Jim Tonge.

There was a fantastic sense of purpose in BARLA in those early days. Everyone was hungry for change and wanted delivery of it. Pretty soon we had district associations or leagues in places most of us had never considered to be rugby league territory. There was certainly enough work to be done when I became the national administrator. We had our offices at the Britannic Building, 3, Upperhead Row, in the middle of Huddersfield, near the bus and railway stations and the George Hotel. At first there was just me and Jean Garside in the office. Jean was a middle-aged, matronly lady with a somewhat Dickensian attitude to office management. We were later joined by Catherine Walker, who became Phil Larder's assistant. At least the Britannic Buildings were easier to get to than Ravensthorpe. To travel there I had needed my 50cc Honda motor-bike. That machine did 100 miles to the gallon, but now I could have gone home for lunch if I wanted to.

# 8. Winning the free gangway

It is no exaggeration to say that I was obsessed with the Rugby Football Union's discriminatory attitude to amateur rugby league players, even before BARLA came into existence. As far as British sport was concerned it would have been hard – well, impossible, really – to find anything more fundamentally unjust than the RFU's ban on amateur rugby league players from playing rugby union once the age of 18 had been passed. Not only that, any rugby union player who had a trial for a professional rugby league club, even if unpaid, would be banned from union for life, unless, of course, the player managed to keep it quiet if they did not switch codes.

In 1972, I made up my mind to try to do something about this injustice and brought the matter to the attention of the local Huddersfield Member of Parliament, Ken Lomas. In turn he put me in touch with other MPs and the Minister of Sport. Michael McGuire, MP for St Helens, also quickly lent his support, and to this day I still see him at matches. His son, Sean, was chief executive at St Helens RLFC.

At the time I was the press officer for the Huddersfield Rugby League Referees Society and had won its support in trying to right this wrong. We all felt that it was simply an injustice that needed sorting out; that it was morally completely indefensible. I probably had not reckoned that sorting it out would take something like 15 years. It was a disgrace that no one in rugby league had even attempted to address the problem in almost 80 years of the game's existence.

The first action I took was to write to the Minister of Sport, Eldon Griffiths. My letter of 18 October, 1972, written from home at High Bank, Exley Lane, Elland, in my capacity as press officer for the Referees Society, pointed out the discrimination involved against amateur rugby league players who were not allowed to play rugby union. It is reproduced in full as an appendix in this book.

A beginning had been made in the fight to bring down rugby's particular form of apartheid, but the struggle was going to be a long, long one. It was clear that rugby union's cage had been rattled a bit, but the big birds were not yet ready to fall off their perches. By August 1973, reports began to appear in the newspapers that Ken Lomas had "won a small victory in his battle for rugby league players to be permitted to play rugby union if they wish." That was all right as far as it went, which, unfortunately, was not very far. The RFU was to ask its clubs to reword their membership application forms in such a way that amateur rugby league players aged over 18 could now ask to join them. Dr Roger Bannister, the first four-minute miler and chairman of the Sports Council, pointed out that some Yorkshire RU clubs had clauses in their application forms implying that rugby league players could not even ask to join union clubs. Under the proposed new wording, a league player would have to state that he had played league and would then have to apply to the RFU for permission to play for or join a rugby union club. Providing he was not a professional he would then be allowed to play union.

At least that was the theory. In practice nothing changed. However, Ken Lomas had also raised before the House of Commons the crucial matter of public funding of amateur sport. He pointed out that Sports Council grants were intended for organisations whose membership was open to everyone and a lot of that money was being wrongly awarded to rugby union clubs, which blatantly discriminated against rugby league players. It would be the scandal of the misuse of public funding that would ultimately prove to be the Achilles heel for the RFU, but we would have a long wait before the final breakthrough.

In the subsequent years, I dealt with a lot of Sports Ministers and chairmen of the Sports Council as BARLA fought for the free gangway between the codes. The struggle gave BARLA an important target which helped tremendously to establish its reputation and prestige in Britain's sporting landscape. We were fighting the Establishment − of society, not of sport. The RFU was part of the Establishment. It had contacts and influence in high places everywhere − unlike the upstarts from BARLA.

One of the frustrating aspects of the fight to get a free gangway was the certain knowledge that locally players had been flouting the RU regulations for years. In Huddersfield we all knew lads who played at Huddersfield RUFC and at Huddersfield YMCA RUFC, who also played league for local clubs. It was the same in lots of other towns and villages across Yorkshire, Lancashire and Cumberland. Sensibly, a lot of officials just turned a blind eye and let the game go on. As long as no one high up in the union hierarchy got to know, these things were tolerated. In the cold light of day, however, some of us deplored the need for any subterfuge at all.

By 1975, BARLA had made considerable progress. There were some pretty big hitters among our leaders, but obviously we were not hitting the RFU hard enough yet.

The RFU leopard had clearly not changed its spots in relation to a genuine free gangway, despite various damaging articles in the press about 'rugby apartheid'. Harold Mather (*The Guardian*), Raymond Fletcher (*Yorkshire Post*) and Jack McNamara (*Manchester Evening News*) had all written strong condemnations of union hypocrisy, but nothing changed. Jack McNamara was particularly obsessive about the subject and had some powerful ammunition to fire when a problem blew up at Siddal in the close season of 1975. In the 1950s there had been end of season knock-out competitions at Rastrick, which encouraged newcomers to play rugby league. They were popular events and a few professionals were allowed to help fill out the teams. Peter Henderson, the former All Black and world class sprinter, and his fellow Fartowner Spanky Dyson were just a couple of the great men who played in those Rastrick knock-outs.

Siddal arranged a gala, a sort of rugby league festival day to raise funds for the club. Part of the gala was a rugby league sevens tournament for players who were new to the game. Four of the lads were members of rugby union clubs who just fancied having a dabble at playing league − not a criminal offence, but a bad move once someone told the RFU. The lads immediately received life-time bans from union and proof that the free gangway was as far away as ever stared us all in face.

I have Jack McNamara's article of 22 September 1975 in my archive and it still makes my blood boil. Under the headline "Time to end feud", Jack wrote: "For sheer vindictiveness, the Rugby Union's unrelenting campaign against rugby league must be unparalleled in sport. Not professional rugby league ... but the amateurs as well.

For all their jolly good sports image, when it comes to rugby league anything goes ... boots, fists and elbows. Any sinner over the age of 18, who has played amateur league, is beyond redemption in union eyes unless he makes a grovelling confession in a bid to get a dispensation. Eighty years after the Northern clubs broke away ... the bitterness lingers on.

Recently, Siddal ... ran a gala sports day to raise money for a children's Christmas party and a new clubhouse. There were swings and donkey rides and a tug-o'-war. There was also a sevens competition for men who had never played rugby league before. Teams had to register nine players and were each allowed two amateurs on the strength. Twelve teams ... entered. There were men who played tennis, cricket, squash and soccer. There were also some union players.

Their clubs heard of this ghastly sin, and this is where the trouble started. 'It appears that they put a block on their players who took part,' says Maurice Oldroyd, the assistant secretary of the British Amateur Rugby League. 'We haven't got a full statement because the clubs say only 'no comment' when asked. The Gala was purely a family affair, and ex-professionals were banned from the sevens'.

How silly can you get? No matter what its archaic laws and bigoted attitudes, the English Union, which is mainly concerned, can no longer justify the barrier against league amateurs.

The League amateurs know they are fighting the establishment and men of immense power and influence, but they are determined to get the stigma of being second-class sporting citizens removed. Northern MPs are helping and are pressing the Sports Council to break the barrier. They have just achieved one major breakthrough – an admission by Minister of Sport, Denis Howell, that discrimination exists. 'What an amateur player cannot do is to switch between the two codes, possibly even playing rugby union on Saturday and rugby league on Sunday', writes Mr Howell to BARLA. 'I wholly deplore this, as I deplore anything which prevents an individual sportsman from participating in the sport of his choice whenever he likes. Ideally, I would like a free gangway between the two codes at the adult amateur level'.

Good for Mr Howell. The Union is hypocritical in its attitude when it welcomes professionals from any other sport, yet bans amateurs because they play another form of rugby.

'What we're fighting for is a free gangway, the sort that exists between every other sport in the country', states Mr Oldroyd. 'An amateur league player shouldn't have to go through the indignity of getting special dispensation to play union, and a union player should be free to play league without the very real fear of excommunication'."

Harold Mather also used the Siddal case in a hard-hitting article in the *Guardian* headed "Amateurs are still blacked by the Union" in April

1976, which was reprinted in the BARLA Handbook. Getting people like Denis Howell on our case helped enormously. A former international soccer referee, he understood sport and was one of the most outstanding ministers of sport that I dealt with, and I dealt with many.

In the 1975 BARLA *Official Handbook* I wrote: "We at BARLA consider such rules [i.e. the RFU's amateur regulations] to be distasteful, against all principles of human dignity and a mockery of amateur sport. Regrettably the RFU go to tremendous lengths to stop the development of our sport. Clear and open attempts have been made to prevent rugby league being established in the universities, with most vehement attacks at the universities of Liverpool, Bradford and Sheffield. All the time it must be remembered that these attacks are against fellow amateurs.

The November issue of *Sportsworld* ... which conducted a special independent investigation into 'Rugby Apartheid', said that the RFU attitude is 'petty and pernicious' and that their case for continuing to bar those who have played amateur Rugby League is 'riddled with anomalies and hypocrisy'.

... Having played both codes, and having many friends in the union game, I can say in all sincerity, that I have yet to meet a union player who agrees with the ban. Unfortunately a few administrators, who appear not only to be hopelessly out of touch with their members, but also the principles and aims of the Sports Council, seem to be totally obsessed with perpetuating a bitter argument of 80 years ago, and in so doing they are souring the very name of rugby – for whether it be league or union, it is in my opinion, the greatest sport in the world."

In the same BARLA *Official Handbook* Tom Keaveney was a touch more vitriolic than me in his Secretary's Annual Report: "Unfortunately, as any rugby fan knows only too well, the Rugby Union bars its members from playing amateur rugby league football after they have reached the age of 18. No doubt many readers can recall known cases of this rather infantile and often pathetic form of discrimination practised by the rugby union establishment in its efforts to belittle the status of our game in the eyes of the general public. Indeed some of the actions and influences used to stop the development of our game, particularly in the universities and south, can only be deplored in the strongest possible terms.

Unfortunately, all polite and reasonable approaches to Twickenham to end this petulant discrimination ... have failed. Indeed the Rugby Union quite arrogantly stated that they had strengthened their rules recently to prevent any 'free gangway' between the two forms of amateur rugby - a remarkable declaration – but clearly indicative of the Rugby Union dogma.

Ken Lomas, MP for Huddersfield, has pointed out in the House of Commons that the foregoing practices place all rugby union clubs in the category of 'private clubs' and as such they are not entitled to the £1 million grant aid which has been given to them over recent years from **public** sources.

The Rugby Union is unique in so far as it is the only national governing body in the country which bars its members from playing another amateur sport and, in so doing, they are flagrantly violating the conditions of grant aid from the Sports Council, of which they are sport's **largest** beneficiary.

Fortunately now, due to the efforts of Mr Lomas and his northern colleagues, perhaps we will see the end of the now infamous 'Rugby Union barrier', and so see our two organisations working together like all other sports, as natural allies and partners in our joint efforts to promote amateur sport. For surely this is what amateur sport is all about – freedom of choice."

Good old Tom.

Another great rugby league man, the late Raymond Fletcher, wrote a telling article in the *Yorkshire Post* on 18 October 1975 which showed how ridiculous it all was: "That the Rugby Union regard the playing of Rugby League as a cardinal sin became obvious a few years ago. Then a convicted murderer serving a life sentence began playing for the prison's Rugby Union side against local teams. All went well for him until it was learned that in his distant past he had played Rugby League. Murder the Rugby Union will forgive, but they could not accept a self-confessed former league player and they gave the unfortunate prisoner their own life sentence."

Raymond also gave the example of a threat to a union club: "In another instance the very future of the century-old Aspatria, Cumbria, rugby union club was threatened when a junior rugby league side sought to share their public park pitch – English Rugby Union rules forbid union players even treading the same turf that has been desecrated by league feet.

Fearing ex-communication, the rugby union club appealed to their Twickenham deity who for once showed mercy and gave the ground their blessing. In their infinite wisdom they decided both clubs could use the same pitch because if it had been forbidden it would have deprived the ratepayers of their entitlement. Amen."

Instances of rugby union's lunatic discrimination could be trotted out *ad nauseam* in those days. One of the worst, again in 1975, was when students at a northern college of education (that is, a teachers' training college) asked Denis Howell to investigate their fear that they would be marked down in their exams if they continued to play amateur rugby league. The student teachers had formed a rugby league side and played friendly games against local youth teams.

Naturally, they approached BARLA for help and Tom Keaveney told the press on 16 July 1975: "They are so afraid of victimisation from the college authorities and the rugby union, that we have given them a pledge not to reveal the name of the college. The college authorities have refused to allow the team to play under the name of the college or on the college playing fields. They have also been told that they will not be allowed to play for the college rugby union teams and the college has threatened that their action in playing rugby league could result in them being banned for life from playing rugby union.

The students' main fear, however, is that if they go openly against the college authorities it could seriously affect their markings in their academic examinations. They would like the government to issue a directive to the college authorities to allow them to openly play amateur rugby league football".

We wrote to Denis Howell about this and to 30 northern MPs requesting help for the students and Tom also wrote to the RFU asking them why, at their recent annual meeting, they had broken their promise to the minister by not discussing rule changes to allow sportsmen to play both amateur codes. The letter accused the RFU of showing "arrogant disdain" to the minister, the government and the Sports Council. I do not recall what the RFU replied, if they even bothered to reply. Their approach to amateur rugby league seemed to consist of gross intimidation on the one hand and a blind belief that in time BARLA would collapse and things would return to 'normal'.

63

Some of the things I have recounted above seem almost surreal now, but then the situation was truly farcical. The RFU just carried on blithely ignoring us or trying to suffocate us. The late Frank Keating interviewed me for *The Guardian* in an article which appeared on 5 April 1977. By then I was the National Administrator for BARLA. He wrote: "Twickenham have only once replied to a number of letters from Maurice Oldroyd … who describes things as Twickenham's 'neurotic obsession of many years to try and kill off rugby league'. He doesn't really expect to have replies – 'They don't like to fraternise or even discuss the matter. And to think that the Sports Council's maxim is that 'all governing bodies should work together as natural allies'." 'Sport for all' was their slogan.

I told Keating of a few other instances of lunacy with which to regale the readers of *The Guardian*, including the case of Reading University's rugby league club. The university authorities offered them a pitch on which the union team also played. When they ran out for their first game they were surprised to find no goal posts. The university union club had dismantled them "on orders from above".

Then there was the matter of Jim Brough's England cap. Brough was a famous full-back for Leeds and captain of the 1936 rugby league Lions. He was a Cumbrian, who had won two England rugby union caps in 1925, while a player with Silloth. Jim was the only man from their club who had ever won an international cap and they asked him to allow them to frame his cap and England jersey and display them in their clubhouse. Jim happily handed the items over, but they had to be taken down once the RFU found out. How petty was that?

Probably just as petty was the case of Bob Mahuta. Bob came from New Zealand to start a post-graduate course in anthropology at Wolfson College, Oxford in 1976. He joined the Oxford Old Boys RU Club and played for them at prop, even though he was 36 years old by then. Back home in Huntly, he had played league at primary school and union at secondary school, gone to university in Auckland and become a head of department at Waikato University.

He had played league as an amateur until he was about 30. The players at Oxford Old Boys knew Bob's background and obviously didn't give a hoot as long as he did his Saturday afternoon stint in their front row. When a league team was formed at Oxford University, Bob started playing for them on Sundays. It was then that he got a letter from his

Old Boys club telling him that the Oxfordshire County RFU had told them he was banned for life from playing union. Questions were raised in Parliament about the ban by Labour MPs Leslie Spriggs (St Helens) and Michael McGuire (Ince). They asked the Sports Minister what he thought about sportsmen being ostracised by a body, the RFU, which received government aid.

Frank Keating wrote in *The Guardian:* "It's not the first time, mind you, that Mr Howell has been asked to defend the indefensible. A couple of years ago, Ken Lomas, another northern Member, asked him why the Sports Council 'were continuing to give money to the Rugby Union – a body that is not open to all the public'. He quoted the Council's grant aid application form, which stated unequivocally that 'no application for membership will be refused … if there be no discrimination on grounds of race, occupation, religion or other opinion'. At the time, the Minister said he would make representation to Twickenham to get the International Board to make changes in their rules. He did so, and the Secretary of the RFU, Bob Weighill, announced smugly that Mr Howell 'seems satisfied that the action we take to maintain our amateur status is reasonable'. Was it pointed out to them that the matter concerned 'amateur' rugby league? The blinkered Union still obviously think they're in the clear. The matter was not so much as mentioned in last week's International Board Meeting – though they did agree to change their rules to allow the amateur Gareth Edwards to receive his four-figure fee for taking part in an American sports competition."

Bob Mahuta took his ban on the chin. He said, "Sure, I was embarrassed at first, both for the Old Boys Club and myself but when you think about it you can only laugh and describe it as just totally ludicrous." Clearly Bob was right. It was ludicrous. Moreover, it was wrong that he should feel embarrassed. He had not committed a crime. The trouble with the RFU was that it simply would not listen to reason. It continued to pretend that rugby league was professional, when BARLA could not have been more true blue amateur.

Eventually things began to move. Pressure was piled on to the RFU via BARLA, the Sport Council, politicians and even the RFL, which gave us good support. David Oxley and the RFL had done the decent thing and recognised BARLA as the independent governing authority for amateur rugby league.

It was totally illogical that one amateur sport could get away with discriminating against another amateur sport. The RFU continued its obstructionist policy, referring matters to the International Board, playing for time, hoping we would give up. The RFU were masters of evasion, hiding things from their members and hiding behind the International Board. It was hard work.

Fortunately, the Sports Council was useful to us simply because it was neutral. During the struggle for the free gangway people like Dickie Jeeps and Peter Yarranton were prominent members of the Sports Council, both former England rugby union internationals. They were big people with influential contacts and I had good relationships with them. There was no acrimony between us but, as I said, the union people I felt were masters of evasion. Things really shifted when John Smith succeeded Jeeps as Chairman of the Sports Council and put his weight behind our cause. He was a millionaire association football man and chairman of Liverpool FC.

I attended some strange meetings with the union people as the struggle for the free gangway progressed. One, in 1985, was at the very posh East India and Devonshire Sporting Club in London. Tom Keaveney and I attended for BARLA, while Bob Weighill was one of those representing the RFU. It was progress, a stepping stone, the first time that they had at least agreed to meet us. It was probably pressure from Westminster that forced them into it. I remember us emphasising our amateur status and ethos, but at the same time acknowledging that the RFU was entitled to make its own regulations regarding professionalism.

I remember another informal meeting (i.e. no minutes were taken) at the Queens Hotel in Leeds, where Eddie Waring used to have his home from home. I was there with Bob Beal (BARLA chairman) and Brigadier Dennis Shuttleworth (RFU president) – all three of us Yorkshiremen. Shuttleworth said, "We can do this one of two ways. We can tackle it head on or we can do nothing – and the latter we're good at." Well, you had to laugh. I thought he was sincere about getting things changed though.

Shuttleworth was right about the RFU's capacity for doing nothing and the struggle for a free gangway rumbled on and on. In 1983 there had been some dispensation for student players, who were allowed to play both games, providing that they had not signed for professional clubs or ever received money for playing. Of course, the RFU did not feel the urge to discriminate against all the players in Wales who received boot money, or the French union players who were paid more than French league players. That would have been a bridge too far.

Although the RFU fought a long and hard rearguard action, the pressure on them was growing from all sides. Apart from BARLA's creeping barrage, the press were increasingly on the case, television documentaries highlighted the injustice, more and more politicians began to take notice and, of course, the Sports Council simply could not let the matter remain unresolved.

A pressure group, Freedom in Rugby, was founded on 30 March 1985 at the George Hotel in Huddersfield, led by Trevor Delaney and Doctor Peter Harrison, specifically to draw attention to the RFU's ridiculous and harmful policies. Two of its members, Martyn Sadler and Lionel Hurst, soon made considerable names for themselves in the game. Freedom in Rugby urged legal action against the RFU because of its continuing acceptance of Sports Council grants under what were clearly false pretences.

At around the same time Ray French, a teacher, former union and league international forward and the BBC's rugby league commentator, was thrown off the Lancashire Rugby Unions Schools' Committee after serving on it for over two decades. He was told he had breached the RFU's regulation 3.9 relating to professionalism. It was a bit rich that they had not noticed during the previous 20 odd years. Ray was considering taking the RFU to court over the matter. It is an understatement to say that things were really hotting up.

The log-jam was ultimately smashed with the threat to stop grants to rugby union. The Sports Council finally insisted that the RFU was in breach of its rules. That was partly in response to the Wigan MP Roger Stott, who had brought up the whole sorry business in Parliament, condemning the RFU's refusal to allow a free gangway, while at the same time pocketing public funds. He had tabled a Parliamentary Early Day Motion on 11 December 1985, calling on the Sports Council to block grants to the RFU until they stopped discriminating against amateur league players. The RFU, as usual, prevaricated, provoking Stott to write to the chairman of the Sports Council, John Smith on 24 February 1986, pointing out that the RFU was in receipt of over £321,000 in capital grants. According to all the rules governing such grants the RFU was in contravention because of its stance against the free gangway.

By October 1986 there was genuine hope that the free gangway would be achieved when the International Rugby Board met but hopes were again dashed. However, six months later at another Board Meeting in London the free gangway was agreed and on 1 May 1987 the newspapers announced that our battle had finally been won. It is hard to explain just how gratified I was to read Paul Fitzpatrick's report in *The Guardian,* the day after the announcement.

Under the headline "League crack union code", he wrote: "Rugby Union's decision to allow a free gangway between itself and amateur rugby league represents a triumph for many people who have striven to bring it about. Above all ... for Maurice Oldroyd ... It is 15 years since Oldroyd wrote to Eldon Griffiths, the then Minister of Sport, stating that 'any amateur sportsman should be free to play as many sports as he chooses at amateur level without fear of prejudice ... rugby union do exercise blatant discrimination against the amateur rugby league player ... He has fought since with enormous patience and considerable diplomacy for a principle: that amateur rugby league players should be allowed the same rights and dignities as every other sportsman in the country. It has been a battle that has taken him into the rarefied atmosphere of air commodores and brigadiers, and there must have been times when he doubted that the divide would ever be bridged. As recently as December 1985, Bob Weighill ... used a full page of *Rugby World* to tell Oldroyd ... why there could be no free gangway."

I received a letter from Dudley Wood, the secretary of the RFU when 'free gangway' had been agreed. He said "I believe that this has long been an anachronism and that the new wording of the regulations is based on common sense." Need one say more!

In the end the issue of public funds proved the RFU's Achilles heel. It was the means to the end. For me it was always the principle of fair play that mattered. BARLA's struggle for the free gangway was a moral issue. We had right on our side. We were always going to win; it was a hell of a struggle, but one I enjoyed. Our achievement was one of the biggest in the history of the politics of British sport.

With Steve Manning (BARLA vice-chair) and Sue Taylor (BARLA chair)
(Photo: David Williams, rlphotos.com)

With David Oxley and Harry Jepson at the President's Ball.

69

With former Huddersfield and Papua New Guinea star Stanley Gene.

With Doctor Dick McConnell at the 2003 Varsity match at Richmond. For many years, Maurice and Dick were the only two people to have seen every Oxford versus Cambridge match.
(Photo: Peter Lush, London League Publications Ltd)

70

# 9. BARLA – 'A sporting success story'

It's funny, but from BARLA's very beginnings I was absolutely confident that the new organisation would be successful. Some people would probably say that was just blind optimism, but what's wrong with optimism? We were lucky in that we had the right people in the organisation and even more blessed that we had a development plan, which was certainly a novelty in rugby league in those days.

Crucially, the new regime at Chapeltown Road more or less left us to our own devices. David Oxley was extremely supportive, the complete opposite of Bill Fallowfield. The mid-1970s seemed like a new world and rugby league appeared to have been bequeathed a fresh start. I like to think that the 'two Os' – Oxley and Oldroyd – were new boys who helped to change things for the better. There were other people from the professional game who were a big help too. Brian Snape, the Salford chairman, became our first president. He was a great man for rugby league. He led the way in promoting the social side of the game, using the Salford club's facilities for entertainment which set a pattern for other clubs to follow and was ahead of his time. He was succeeded for a couple of years by Bradford Northern's Harry Womersley before Bob Beal, from an amateur rugby league background, took the presidency in 1978.

Ronnie Simpson (Castleford) and Sumner Baxendale (Wigan) were early BARLA vice-presidents, while that fantastic Huddersfield stalwart Hubert Lockwood quietly helped BARLA a lot behind the scenes. Hubert was a real gentleman with a lot of influence and was chairman of the Rugby League Council from 1970 to 1972. Apart from being a fine administrator, Hubert was a record-breaking goalkicking full-back for Halifax in the 1930s and 1940s – a great all-round rugby league man.

Although it was hard work for all concerned, BARLA flourished dramatically on a wave of enthusiasm and ambition. In fact things went so well that the Sports Council often referred to BARLA as a national "sporting success story". Another catch phrase began to stick to BARLA – "join BARLA and see the world". That was a reference to the huge growth the new organisation brought to rugby league tours and world-wide expansion. Prior to BARLA's foundation, all the RFL provided in international terms for amateur players were annual open-age and under-19s internationals against France.

71

Two rugby league legends, both admired by Maurice for their contribution to the sport.

Left: Tom Mitchell, who was always a great supporter of BARLA.

Below: Eddie Waring.

(Both photos: Courtesy Robert Gate)

We carried on playing France annually, sometimes twice, at open-age and youth level, but our horizons were much broader than a jaunt across the Channel every couple of years. Very soon BARLA was sending tours to the other side of the world.

In June 1977 we despatched a Great Britain youth squad to New Zealand and Australia – what a breakthrough that was for amateur rugby league. The tour managers were Dougie Hird and Alan Lancaster and five games were played. In the internationals we drew 11–11 with a New Zealand XIII in Christchurch and lost 21–13 to an Australian XIII in Sydney. Both of those games were played as curtain-raisers to World Cup games involving the Great Britain professional team, the latter before the World Cup Final itself against Australia at the Sydney Cricket Ground. Our performance against the Australian XIII was particularly impressive when you bear in mind that there were 10,000 youth teams in Australia. We had a few hundred youth teams. The captain of that BARLA youth squad was the Simms Cross stand-off Terry McGovern, a fantastic honour in rugby league history. Some of the lads who were in the squad became famous in the professional game – David Hobbs (Featherstone Rovers), Nicky Kiss (Wigan) and David Cairns (Barrow), for example, became test players.

That tour owed a lot to the efforts of Dougie Hird. He had apparently already been planning to take his club Shaw Cross out to Australia on a ground-breaking tour. When I discussed the matter with him and brought up the idea of a BARLA tour down under, he said: "Tell you what. We'll take a squad of 20 players and two officials. We'll have two Shaw Cross players in the party and the rest can be selected on merit." You had to take Dougie seriously; he had years of experience organising Shaw Cross tours to France. In fact, Shaw Cross are still touring France or receiving French visitors every year. Mary was the official translator for the Shaw Cross-French jamborees for many years. The club had to raise the funds itself for those tours until the Sports Council eventually gave them some help with grants. The great work done by enthusiasts like Dougie Hird in the old days should not be forgotten. They did not get anything on a plate.

The Queen's Silver Jubilee celebrations coincided with that tour in 1977 and in the same year BARLA was recognised by the presentation of Queen's Silver Jubilee Medals to five of the amateur game's leading administrators. Bob Beal, Tom Beautiman, Jack Clayton, Edgar Hanson and Ernie Houghton were the honoured men. That national recognition was a big boost for the amateur game, as was the £40,000 grant aid which the Sports Council pumped into BARLA in the 1976–77 season.

I think it is fair to say that BARLA had come a long way in a short time. We established a National Cup competition in 1973–74, when Leigh Miners Welfare beat Latchford Albion 12–7 in the final. We also created a National Youth Cup at the same time with Milford winning the first final rather more easily: 49–0 against Ince. National Sevens competitions at open-age and youth levels were also inaugurated in that season. The first winners were Hemsworth Miners Welfare and Saddleworth Rangers respectively.

By 1977, we had our own headquarters at Upperhead Row in Huddersfield, which was opened officially by Minister of Sport Denis Howell on 13 September. I remember Howell coming in for some flak in those days, outside of his sporting responsibilities. First he was charged with being Minister for Drought and then Minister for Floods – a man for all seasons, really.

I have among my piles of news cuttings an article by Paul Fitzpatrick from *The Guardian* dated 23 February 1978, which accurately reflects BARLA's progress. He wrote: "Before the advent of the British Amateur Rugby League Association in 1973, amateur rugby league, though still vigorous in the schools, was in general in a chronic state, disorganised, ill-disciplined, dying. In less than five years a remarkable change has been wrought. A flourishing sport is now played by at least 80,000 amateurs, students and schoolboys. Oxford University, no less, have a side; Cambridge University are in the process of following suit. The not unjustified image of amateur rugby league being an excuse for a brawl has been replaced by one of healthy vitality and respectability.

I always look forward to the annual Varsity match. The first game was at Fulham in 1981. I went with David Oxley. The most recent was the 34th match, and it was played in the City of London, at the Honourable Artillery Company ground. To me, the top man involved is Dr Dick McConnell. He is a New Zealander, and played in the first game for Cambridge, and has been involved ever since. But I'm the only person to have seen every match; Dick missed one when he was stranded in New York. Dick is a lovely man, and still very active in the game.

For rugby league, Oxford versus Cambridge has a lot of social status. It's important for the sport – 'climbing the ladder' if you like. It brings people in the establishment into contact with rugby league. Our code was frowned upon years ago in places like Oxford and Cambridge, and establishing this match was a breakthrough for the sport. I went with David Oxley to the last game, he was there as President of the RFL. The standard of the game is good, it's very competitive and means a lot to the players.

When student rugby league started in the late 1960s, I refereed some of the early matches, even though they were on Wednesday afternoons. I did not have to work on Wednesdays, and thoroughly enjoyed them. I used to do the Leeds Polytechnic and Carnegie matches. Martyn Sadler, the editor of *League Express*, was involved in developing student rugby league.

Curiously, BARLA, like the Rugby League itself in 1895, began life as an outcast. At a meeting of the Rugby League Council in 1973 only one man, the singular Tom Mitchell, whose forceful, bearded countenance now gazes down from the walls of BARLA's offices in Huddersfield, was in favour of the new body. Early life was thus hard for the shunned infant, orphaned before it was walking, unrecognised by the Rugby League and thus by the government and the Sports Council also.

Attitudes, however, can change swiftly and when Maurice Oldroyd ... outlined the aims and ambitions of BARLA at another meeting of the Rugby League Council in Salford in 1974, the mood had changed from one of almost total opposition to unanimous support. Many people in the game now feel that that blessing given to BARLA was one of the most significant decisions the [RFL has] ever taken. Not only was amateur rugby rescued, but possibly the professional game as well.

BARLA have made scarcely the suggestion of an error since. Oldroyd gave up a secure, executive job in industry to become BARLA's first full-time official, but has never regretted his decision. It is Oldroyd's objective to see amateur rugby league played throughout the British Isles by 1995 and the missionary zeal which he and everyone else connected with the amateur game are pursuing their visions make that objective credible. Although the game is still confined mainly to the north new leagues are being formed all the time. BARLA, says Oldroyd, are on schedule."

I am not quite sure of Paul's assertion that the creation of BARLA may have saved the professional game as well as the amateur game, but he was certainly right about BARLA's other achievements. By 1978 our full member leagues comprised Barrow, Bradford, Castleford, Cumberland, Doncaster, Halifax, Heavy Woollen, Huddersfield, Kingston-upon-Hull and Humberside, Leeds, Leigh, Manchester, Oldham, Rochdale, St Helens, Wakefield, Warrington, Widnes, Wigan and York. We also had in membership the English Schools Rugby League, Humberside Youth League, Southern Amateur Rugby League and University and College Rugby League Clubs Association.

Moreover, we had associate member leagues in the Bradford and Keighley Youth League, Kirklees Youth League, Scottish Amateur Rugby League Youth Association and Southern Schools and Youth Clubs Amateur Rugby League Association. Of course, all this took a lot of organising and we were all pleased when BARLA's secretary Tom Keaveney was awarded the MBE in the Queen's Birthday Honours List in June 1978.

There was another major landmark in 1978 when BARLA organised an open-age tour to Papua New Guinea, Australia and New Zealand. Really this was a quite mind-boggling achievement bearing in mind where we had started out from just a few years earlier. This time we sent out a party of 26 players and six officials, including a coach, the redoubtable Sam Morton from Dewsbury Celtic. The captain was Bob Colgrave, a cracking forward with Ace Amateurs (Hull). These lads were real amateurs. Most of them were going to miss six weeks paid work to undertake an itinerary of nine matches in 32 days, five of which were in Papua. They would also have to pay £40 for their tour suits and the only thing they got free from BARLA was a BARLA tie. The Sports Council came up trumps with a grant of £17,000, while BARLA had to raise another £10,000. That was a hell of a lot of money, but we raised it.

I always think that the 1978 tour was truly historic. Even today, it's incredible to think that young men from Yorkshire, Lancashire and Cumbria, were able to visit such exotic places as Papua New Guinea as amateur rugby league players. The world was certainly changing.

By all accounts the Papuan section of the tour was amazing. There were capacity crowds for all the games there and BARLA won the only test match 28–7 in Port Moresby. All those tales about people climbing

76

trees outside the grounds to get a view of the games are true. In fact Papuans were so besotted with rugby league that our PRO Ray Dennett reported that for the game at Mount Hagen, some people had walked 200 miles to see the clash against Highlands. BARLA won that game 26–25. Sadly, the previous game at Lae against Northern Zone had to be abandoned with six minutes left after about 400 people invaded the pitch and attacked the players. The players had to lock themselves in the dressing rooms. Ray Dennett's headline was "The charge of the Light Brigade". Before the party went to Mount Hagen our officials wanted some assurances about safety, but some of the Papuan officials said they could not make any guarantees, because "the people up there are not civilised like we are in Rabaul."

In later years, I went to Rabaul on International Board duty for BARLA, but I never went on a BARLA tour. That was just for coaches and managers. While I was in Rabaul I went to a match and went for a stroll around the ground perimeter, resplendent in my maroon BARLA blazer – a real eye-catcher. I was amazed to be applauded all the way round with the crowd chanting "BARLA! BARLA!"

Mention of the 1978 tour brings to mind a special player, Steve Critchenson. I often think he was the most impressive amateur rugby league player I ever saw. He was certainly my favourite amateur player. Steve, a brilliant winger for Ace Amateurs, was in the squad. He was a heck of a winger. In the lead-up to the tour he had played for Great Britain against France at Workington. Amateur internationals against France were not easy and the French France tended to win more than they lost. Not on this occasion though, because Steve crashed over for three tries in a 36–7 rout. I also recall that he scored hat-tricks in some other big games such as the National Cup Final for Ace and a National Inter-League Final for Hull ARL. Lots of professional clubs tried to sign Steve, but he always turned them down because he wanted to play soccer on Sunday mornings and, besides, his work on North Sea oilrigs would make things complicated.

BARLA had begun to raise standards across the board; so much so that some of our amateur clubs could give the professionals a run for their money. I like to think it was amateurs raising their standards, rather than the professionals lowering theirs, although it has to be admitted that the professional game had been in the doldrums.

77

The BARLA Management Committee with Denis Howell MP, who was Minister for Sport and Recreation in the 1974 to 1979 Labour Government.

With Jack Brook (Mayor of Kirklees), Betty Boothroyd MP (speaker of the House of Commons and Winnie Kane (Mayoress of Kirklees).

1993 International Board meeting in Queensland: With Mary and Maurice are
John McDonald, Gilbert Dutin and Bob Abbot.

The 1983 Maori tour. With Maurice and Mary are Tony Wright,
Tom Newton and Ray Oldfield. BARLA played the Maori team.

In 1977 Cawoods (also known as West Hull) had produced a real turn-up by winning 9–8 at Halifax in the first round of the John Player Trophy. It was the first time an amateur club had knocked out a professional club in a major cup competition since 1909, when Beverley had beaten Ebbw Vale. Admittedly, Halifax were bottom of the league, but it was still a great performance by Cawoods.

There was nothing bottom-of-the-league about Wigan and Castleford though, who both came up against Pilkington Recs from St Helens in the first round of the Challenge Cup in 1977 and 1978. Pilks were in those days, I think, just about the best amateur team I ever saw. In 1977 Wigan scraped home 10–4.

In 1978, Pilks were just pipped 23–22 by Castleford. Billy Thompson refereed that match and I seem to recall him saying that Mal Reilly looked really worried when standing behind the posts after a Pilks' try had put Cas behind. When he trotted back to the half-way line with Billy for the kick-off, he said: "We'd better not bloody lose this game. Trouble is they're the better team so far." Of course, Cas just got out of jail in the end, but if they had not, would Malcolm have still had a job the following week? Makes you wonder, doesn't it? Both games were played at Knowsley Road, the game against Wigan attracting a crowd of around 11,000 when rugby league rarely attendances of that size.

Tom Keaveney and I did get to visit some interesting places when we attended International Board meetings. We went Paris, Papua, Australia and New Zealand, but it was a bit of a let-down one year when we only got as far as Walton Hall, near Wakefield. Walton Hall was a first class venue for a conference, set in lovely parkland with a magnificent lake, but we could have caught a service bus to get there.

David Oxley was also attending and I don't think he quite got the joke when I asked him "Why have the RFL organised it for Wakefield? Somehow it hasn't the same allure as Paris, Auckland or Sydney." I had to reassure him that I was not questioning his organisational abilities.

There were some very interesting people at International Board meetings. At one the chairman was Kevin Humphreys, a really tough Australian, who later almost brought the game in Australia to its knees in a big scandal. At that particular IB meeting Humphreys was in such complete control as chairman that I turned to Tom and said: "If Humphreys suggests we change to two-a-side rugby, all the delegates' hands will shoot up like pistons." I felt it was a blessing when Ken

Arthurson eventually took over from Kevin Humphreys as chairman of the ARL in 1983.

BARLA continued to break new ground. In 1979 we invited Papua New Guinea to this country for the first time. They played games at St Helens, Barrow and Hull. The latter game was a test at The Boulevard and BARLA won well – 28–12. That was quite a coup as the Papuans had beaten France Under-24s 14–4 in Toulouse and gave the full French test team two close games in Albi and Carcassonne. For each of the games in England we invited the local mayors and other council officials because we realised that involving the local community was a vital element in raising our profile. We were clearly ahead of our time.

A novel feature of the games was the Papuans' performances of cultural rituals and traditional dances – pre-match entertainment long before Super League. The tour was made more special for me because the executive manager of the tour Tony Lavutui presented me with Life Membership of the Papua New Guinea Rugby League in recognition of my work in pioneering the two historic tours between our countries. It was a very gratifying gesture.

Apparently I was only the third European to be so honoured. The others were Rene Mauries, the president of the French Rugby League, and, ironically enough, Bill Fallowfield, who was at that time secretary of the International Board. There is a picture of me receiving the Life Membership and a Papua RL tie from Tony Lavutui in the *BARLA Official Handbook* for 1980–81. I wish my hair was still that dark.

Another touring team arrived in England a bit unexpectedly in 1979. I was in the office when the phone rang. It was Arthur Clues – Big Arthur, the famous and infamous Australian second-rower who was a legend with Leeds and Hunslet in the 1940s and 1950s. He had stayed in Leeds after finishing playing and ran a sports outfitting business. Everyone in rugby league knew Arthur and when he spoke they listened. He said "I see you are promoting international rugby league." I replied "Yes, we're doing our best. What can I do for you?" Arthur carried on "I've got an Australian team wanting a game." I asked "When are they coming?" His response was "They're already effing here." Arthur did a lot of swearing.

I told Arthur I would get back to him. The team he was talking about was Tweed Heads Seagulls, a country club from New South Wales. They were amateurs and their club ran 14 teams in 10 age groups as well as a first and reserve side. It was a bit of a poser. The Seagulls had simply arrived in England unannounced, an amazing thing to do. I managed to fix up a game for them against my old club, Underbank, at Fartown. They were a bit too sharp and organised for Underbank and won 19–5, but it was a good game. This was the first time an Australian amateur rugby league club had ever been to Britain. It was another historic first for BARLA, albeit not exactly of our making. The Seagulls fancied a trip to Blackpool so we arranged for them to play ICI Thornton and after they had done that they went to France. Heaven knows what they did there.

By 1980, BARLA was on a roll. The changes and improvements had been massive and showed no real signs of slowing. By then we had added to our membership the Barnsley Amateur Rugby League, the West Yorkshire ARL (six divisions), the Yorkshire ARL (three divisions) and two organisations which would become giants of the amateur game, the Pennine ARL containing seven divisions and the North West Counties ARL, which had five divisions and additional leagues for under-19s, under-17s and under-16s. In the 1980—81 season one of our clubs, Shevington Sharks from Wigan, became the first club to tour the United States, and won all four games they played.

The Australian Combined High Schools visited Europe in January and beat the BARLA Great Britain Youth team 14–2 at Headingley on a massively successful tour. We knew that the Australian Schoolboys would be difficult to beat because a similarly successful Australian Schools party had been over to Britain in 1972.

Of course, not everything was perfect. In October 1980 BARLA and the RFL became embroiled in a big row over the running of under-17 teams. The RFL had decided to start a youth league and 10 supporters club teams, consisting of junior players, from the professional clubs began to operate. As far as BARLA was concerned, this was against our agreement with the RFL. Matters escalated and the RFL decided to withhold various grants from BARLA. Lots of people within the professional clubs were on BARLA's side and it was extremely ironic when Bill Fallowfield, our old enemy, took our side. He told Jack McNamara in the *Manchester Evening News* that his experience had shown that the RFL should leave the amateur game entirely to BARLA. That was quite a turnaround by Bill.

82

Albert Fearnley, the RFL's joint head of the National Coaching Scheme, was another big hitter who advised the RFL to leave youth rugby to BARLA. The dispute rumbled on for over a year before it was amicably settled. The professional clubs agreed to a structure of playing a first team, reserves ('A' teams), and a Colts team (under-19s). Youth rugby would be left to BARLA. Periodically, there have been similar spats and it is a fact of rugby league life that youth rugby has been the biggest bone of contention between amateurs and professionals.

One of the most crucial boosts to the promotion of rugby league was the National Coaching Scheme. The RFL had run its own coaching scheme for many years with Albert Fearnley and Laurie Gant in charge. They had some good coaches under them running the regions too. Tommy Dawes, the old Barrow full-back, was responsible for Cumbria. Arthur Bunting, formerly a super scrum-half with Hull KR, was in charge of Humberside, while Mick Naughton, the international referee from Widnes, looked after the North West Counties. Yorkshire had two regional coaches in Maurice Bamford (East Pennine) and Paul Daley (West Yorkshire), while Graham Starkey covered the West Pennine region. It was a good set up, but it was about to get even better.

Relations with the RFL got back on an even keel and a BARLA-RFL joint liaison committee began to meet every three months. In 1982 BARLA, the RFL and the Sports Council agreed that the coaching scheme should embrace the whole game. There was considerable thought going into the technical aspects of sport skills, preparation and coaching in those days and we all agreed rugby league should not be left behind. The Sports Council, with its motto 'Sport for All' ringing in everyone's ears, provided a grant to help fund a new National Coaching Scheme, and particularly to fund a full-time director of coaching. That would be a pivotal appointment in the development of the game. Moreover, it was another example of bringing public money into the game, which would have been inconceivable before the birth of BARLA because in those days the Sports Council's focus was on amateur sport, volunteers and mass participation. They were not there to prop up professional sports clubs.

It was essential to get the right man for the job and BARLA had a particular interest in who that might be, as he would be based at our headquarters in Huddersfield. The lucky man was Phil Larder, who beat

83

a field of about 40 applicants. Phil proved to be the right man. He had played both codes of rugby to a high level, and had earned a 10 year testimonial for Oldham. He was still young and playing for Whitehaven.

I think I told him it was time to stop playing. Phil was a teacher. He was also chairman of the British Upper Schools and Colleges Amateur Rugby League Association (BUSCARLA), which had recently been founded and was an associated member league of BARLA. So he had a good pedigree – teaching skills, knowledge of school systems and an intimate acquaintance with the workings of professional rugby league. He was intelligent and articulate – a good man for changing times.

Under Phil the National Coaching scheme was modernised and streamlined. Many more coaches were produced and just as importantly they were now properly and officially qualified coaches. Phil was also involved in coaching and preparing the Great Britain team at professional level, as well as having spells with Keighley Cougars, Sheffield Eagles and Widnes. Of course, he became more famous after he left rugby league for rugby union. He was appointed as defence coach for England and helped them to win the World Cup in 2003. Another BARLA product was one of the stars of that World Cup-winning side: Jason Robinson, who started off with Hunslet Parkside ARL.

BARLA also introduced development officers whose work dovetailed nicely with the coaches. Our first full-time development officer was Maurice Bamford in Leeds, who was part funded by Leeds City Council and part by BARLA, but I dare say most people will remember him more for his moustache and his coaching. If ever a man loved rugby league, it was Maurice.

BARLA was definitely getting most things right in the 1980s. We had sorted out our administration, coaching and development. In other words our structure was sound. Our leagues and competitions were strong. The county cup competitions were popular and our National Cup competition was massive. We also attracted good sponsors and generated a lot of publicity in the press and through local radio stations. We had introduced a BARLA Player of the Year trophy and a BARLA Youth Player of the Year trophy very early in our existence and some great players had won the awards. These initiatives generated a lot of interest and publicity which was all positive. It was measurable too. In 1982 we had 700 teams and 18,000 players. Four years later we had 800 teams and 20,000 players. By 1990, 1,100 teams were registered with BARLA and it was estimated that almost 50,000 players – amateurs and schoolboys – were in action on an average weekend. I think that could be called progress.

On a wider front, by 1990 amateur rugby league was played in 16 countries, compared to the mere five when BARLA was founded. The decade had seen BARLA open age tours to Papua New Guinea and Australia in 1982, to Australia in 1986 and to Western Samoa, Tonga and the Cook Islands in 1990.Youth tours had gone to New Zealand in 1983 and Australia in 1989, while BUSCARLA toured Australia in 1984 and there had been a University World Cup in New Zealand in 1986. Inbound tours to the UK comprised New Zealand Maoris (open age, 1983), New Zealand Universities (under-23s, 1984), Australian Schoolboys (1986), New Zealand Junior Kiwis (Youth, 1987), Papua New Guinea (open age, 1987) and the Student World Cup (under-23s, 1989).

In 1983 the Welsh Amateur Rugby League Association (WARLA) was founded and two years later the Midlands and South West Amateur Rugby League Association (MASWARLA) and the North East Amateur Rugby League Association (NEARLA) appeared. Amateur clubs were springing up all over Britain. It was all quite staggering considering that BARLA had started with a membership of 155 teams and just £25 in the bank. By 1990 we had declared our intention to making amateur rugby league a truly national sport by the time the centenary of the game came round in 1995. The Sports Council had earmarked £640,000 for us between 1990 and 1995 and it looked as if we were right on course to achieve our aims.

In 1986 BARLA's National Cup attracted a world record entry for a rugby league competition of 164 teams. By 1990 that figure had grown to 221 teams and was thought to be a world record for either form of rugby. 1986 was also a momentous year for the amateur game as a new National League of 10 top clubs was inaugurated. Three years later it was extended to two divisions and 22 clubs. It was phenomenally successful and in 1990 attracted an unprecedented sponsorship of £100,000 over three seasons from British Coal Opencast. The National League, dubbed by many newspapers "the Super League", eventually became the National Conference League, the amateur game's flagship competition comprising three leagues, with excellent playing standards and requiring set standards off the

85

field. That same year two grants earned by BARLA showed just how far the Association had come. We were given £180,000 by Greater Manchester Council to develop the game's first purpose-built Centre of Excellence at Leigh and another £150,000 grant from West Yorkshire Metropolitan Council to help us fund new headquarters for BARLA. We might have been amateurs, but we were far from being amateurish.

The Leigh Centre of Excellence was opened in 1988, but our move to new headquarters took a little longer. However, we did not have to move far – just a little higher up the road and almost within kicking distance of the George Hotel, where the Northern Union came into being in 1895. It was never intended that we should move out of Huddersfield, which, in my opinion, has always been the most appropriate place for us in view of its historic links with the game. Our new headquarters were at West Yorkshire House, a colossal, new, detached building. It was very impressive compared to our former home at the Britannic Buildings.

One of the things I loved about my job was that it was not nine to five by any stretch of the imagination. For me it was all enveloping. I knew I was a lucky man. Tom Keaveney was still the BARLA secretary and operated from his home. He was a wonder, being still secretary of the Pennine League and secretary of the Huddersfield League. If we needed to go anywhere together, we went in Tom's car. The work was interesting and all sorts cropped up and needed to be dealt with. Under my development remit I went round local councils paving the way for the establishment of development officers. I got used to dealing with Members of Parliament, Ministers of Sport, local authorities and communities. Tom and I would not always agree about things, but the game came first and we were both lucky to have such super and supportive wives.

All this experience served me well in my work on the International Board on which I served for a quarter of a century. I may have been its longest serving member, unless my good friend and colleague from New Zealand Ron McGregor beat me for that distinction.

By 1989 when we moved into West Yorkshire House we had, from my hazy memory, about nine members of staff. Ian Cooper, a very competent operator, had been appointed administrative officer, Phil Larder was running the coaching scheme and Tom O'Donovan, a former Mayor of Kirklees, had been brought in as national development officer. In addition, there was excellent secretarial and administrative expertise in the shape of Bev Meadows, Tracey Bentley, Carla Carney, Kathy Taylor and Katherine Walker.

Although West Yorkshire House had been opened in 1989, something had been bubbling in my mind. I thought that getting our own headquarters should be commemorated by something special. So, with Mary's support, I decided we should invite the Queen to see our new home. One day soon afterwards one of our office staff collared me and said, "There are a couple of gentlemen wanting to see the office." For some reason I assumed they were from the council and proceeded to show them round. In passing I said "Actually I have invited the Queen to officially open our offices". One of them replied: "Mr Oldroyd, that's why we are here today." I am not kidding when I say it was a total surprise. They were security men acting under the authority of the Lord Lieutenant of West Yorkshire.

So, to use an old cliché, BARLA was given the royal seal of approval. The Queen's visit had been scheduled for 30 November 1990. She arrived in a Rolls Royce, the Royal Ensign fluttering, and the streets around were packed solid. I remember soldiers of the Duke of Wellington's Regiment ran the Royal Standard up our flagpole. I also remember that there were men with guns on the roof of St Patrick's Club, the building opposite West Yorkshire House. The daughter of our president, David Knight, presented flowers to the Queen and Tom Mitchell, BARLA's Patron, was introduced to her, followed by all the staff. It was a lovely occasion and there was lunch for about 30 people in the BARLA executive suite. However, there was a bit of a fright when during the meal the fire alarm went off. Some of us were ready to panic, but not the Queen, who was sitting with BARLA chairman Alan Gibb. She turned to him and said, "Don't worry, Mr Gibb. If there is any danger, they will get us out." Within seconds two security men completely blocked the door. The alarm was sorted out and no one was killed. The Queen stayed longer than anticipated so she must have enjoyed her visit. Apparently she never tugged at the handbag of her lady-in-waiting, which was the secret sign to draw matters to a conclusion when she had had enough. Mary was present of course, along with stacks of photographers, and Tom Mitchell took on the job of guiding the Queen around the building. Knowing Tom, with all his connections, he probably knew her quite well.

Apart from the fire alarm incident, everything went off well while she was with us. Her visit was probably the best publicity BARLA could hope for and we certainly felt that the association had arrived as a significant player in the sporting world.

That evening there was an open reception for anyone who wanted to see the new offices. For the occasion we had borrowed a painting of Hannah Hauxwell by Peter Brook, a very famous artist with local connections. In fact, Mary and I had quite a lot of pictures by Peter and knew him well, because he was the art master at Sowerby Bridge Grammar School. This particular painting was massive and covered half the wall in the boardroom. We only had it for the day and it was insured for £30,000. You can probably imagine my horror when I went into the boardroom and there was no painting to be seen. Fortunately, it had not been stolen. Someone had taken it down and put it in a safe place. It was quite a shock for me though. I could have had a heart attack. Not exactly a perfect end to an otherwise perfect day.

Arriving at BARLA – the start of a successful visit.

Unveiling the plaque that commemorated the visit.

Her Majesty signing the visitors' book.

Visiting the display that outlined the history of BARLA.

Receiving a rugby league ball – a souvenir of the visit.

Her Majesty meeting Harry Jepson, as Tom Mitchell waits in line. On the left are Ron McGregor and his wife, from New Zealand. Ron was the International Board President.

Mary and Maurice checking that everything is in place.

# 10. Towards the Millennium

While the royal visit to BARLA in 1990 may in hindsight perhaps be seen as the pinnacle of the organisation's existence, there was still much to be done. Success accompanied the amateur game for several years to come, but the game was soon to hit stormy waters and BARLA was not exempt from the damage which gushed forth.

As the 1990s began many in the world of rugby league were looking forward to the game's centenary in 1995. Indeed, as I said earlier, BARLA had set its sights on trying to spread the amateur game to all parts of England by 1995 and to make inroads into the rest of Britain. The decade had begun with a seven-match BARLA open age tour to the Cook Islands, Western Samoa and Tonga in May and June. That was followed by a record £100,000 sponsorship of BARLA by British Coal Opencast over three years, which began in August 1990.

Between 1990 and Centenary Year BARLA organised youth tours to New Zealand in 1991 and 1995, and Australia in 1993; an under-23 tour to South Africa in 1994 and open age tours to Western Samoa, Tonga, Cook Islands and Fiji in 1994 and South Africa in 1995. We welcomed tours from the Australian Schoolboys in 1991 and from New Zealand Junior Kiwis in 1993, both of which played our youth teams. In March 1994, our Great Britain youth team broke new ground in beating Morocco 48–14 in Casablanca, while at open age level BARLA Great Britain beat Russia twice, and Moldova in April and May of 1994. BARLA was pushing the game's boundaries.

Most of the £100,000 Opencast sponsorship was directed to the elite National Leagues, which now consisted of 24 clubs in two divisions. Beverley and Greetland All-Rounders were added to the second division in 1990. I was very pleased that Greetland gained admission as that's where we lived and their ground was just up the road from us. The National League was BARLA's flagship competition; all its clubs had to meet strict requirements relating to their ground, social facilities, youth set-up and playing standards. In its own way it was a form of franchising before anyone had dreamed of Super League. In 1993 it was renamed the National Conference League and operated three divisions (Premier, First and Second). Standards of play in the NCL rose over the years until some of its clubs bore favourable comparison with the bottom division of the professional game.

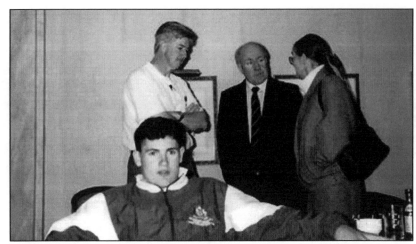
1991 Australian Schoolboys tour: Maurice and Mary with Brian Pearson.

Ready to speak in 1991.

With Alan Gibb, Brian Pearson and a local mayor in 1991.

Left: With Ron McGregor at an International Board meeting.

Middle: Adam and Ron McGregor in 2002.

Bottom: With Mary at Elland – Riorges 20th anniversary in 1998.

Of all the problems BARLA faced in its relations with the RFL, youth rugby was always the most prickly. By the early 1990s BARLA had been going for almost two decades and some people seemed to have forgotten how under-funded, un-respected and invisible the game at junior levels had been before 1973.

Also, some of the professional clubs seemed to have little regard for their debts to the amateur clubs, which, when all was said and done, produced around 90 per cent of the players who filled their ranks. In 1990 the professional clubs between them owed BARLA and its member clubs £6,000 in unpaid signing fees. It only cost a professional club £50 to register an amateur signing, £40 of which was to the BARLA club and £10 to BARLA. It was hardly a fortune, considering how much might be paid to a convert from rugby union. Welsh RU capped players would be getting thousands of pounds, for example, and they had never even played rugby league. That issue was a running sore and until very recently it was still running.

However, compared to what happened in the summer of 1991, it seemed fairly inconsequential, even if it was patently indefensible. A bitter dispute developed when the RFL decided to create an Academy competition without bothering to consult BARLA, which had been given complete autonomy for running the entire amateur game on 26 September 1974. That agreement had been signed by the RFL and approved by the Sports Council. Four years later, on 29 December 1978, the National Coaching Scheme was transferred to BARLA and operated from BARLA HQ.

In 1991 the RFL unilaterally declared they were taking over the National Coaching scheme and Phil Larder, its director, moved with it to an office in the RFL's Chapeltown Road HQ. Soon after this happened I turned up at Chapeltown Road to attend a meeting of the National Coaching Scheme and someone decided I should not be admitted. It got a bit comical, as I was a determined little so-and-so. I sidestepped the first tackle and then one of the RFL officials attempted to lift me out of the place. In the process I got a bit of bruising under the jaw for my pains.

At the time I remember thinking to myself, "They can't even stop a little half-back". I don't know why I had such a thought. It was different from the usual day in the office. I have, by the way, always got on well with the RFL person involved, so I didn't sue him.

Naturally, many people in the amateur game were very upset and Tom Keaveney was positively incandescent. In his national secretary's report for 1992 he declared: "In January 1991 we contacted the RFL with a view to planning youth rugby for the season 1991–92, having almost come to the end of the agreed three years British Coal sponsorship. The Rugby Football League refused to meet us until June. It was at this meeting we were advised that the Rugby Football League were going to launch the Academy and they did not think any discussion or consultation appropriate. What arrogance. Despite eleventh-hour efforts to [persuade them] to re-think the consequences of their actions, which included addressing the Rugby League Council and a letter from the Sports Council advising the RFL to open a dialogue, the RFL pressed on regardless. The rest is history. An horrendous and totally unnecessary period of confrontation yet again."

Besides the RFL establishing their Academy Tom also pointed out, "They also made the Students, English schools and Civil service Associate Members of the Rugby Football League. All this was done without any consultation with BARLA, the governing body for the amateur game … No-one should be duped by the fact that all the actions of the RFL are for the good of the game. This is utter nonsense. Had the RFL been genuine in their good-of-the-game syndrome, they would have held talks with BARLA before they took the actions they did. No, this whole dispute is about control. There is no doubt the RFL are keen to control the amateur game from under-19 downwards for their own ends – not for the good of the game."

Tom was spot on about the whole dispute being about control. Ever since the foundation of BARLA our nurturing of the youth game had been the jewel in our crown, our prime function in fact. We regarded the Academy as undermining our thriving youth policies and disruptive to our progress in developing young players. Of course, it has always been understandable that the professional clubs want players quickly and off the peg. The game needed an agreed system beneficial to all and that is what we believed BARLA provided. When all was said and done, we were proud to provide the professional game with the vast majority of its players, but that was not our main objective.

The spat that erupted in 1991 turned nasty pretty quickly. BARLA decided to ban any players who took part in the Academy, effectively declaring them professionals, which to many people smacked of the old rugby union attitude to league. The RFL responded by withdrawing their normal invitations to amateur clubs to compete in the Challenge Cup and Regal Trophy. Things then seemed to calm down and both sides withdrew their sanctions and by January 1992 an announcement was made that "the RFL and BARLA had reached an agreement on unification." David Oxley told the press: "It is one of the most momentous decisions since the breakaway from the English Rugby Union in 1895 and certainly the most important policy-making decision." Unfortunately, David was a bit premature on that score.

The summer of 1992 saw the whole thing flare up again, more sanctions were imposed by BARLA against Academy players and the RFL banned BARLA clubs from using professional clubs' grounds. By October the Sports Council offered to arbitrate between the warring factions and eventually negotiations led by Maurice Lindsay, the new CEO of the RFL, and Peter Moran, BARLA's president, led to an agreement in 1993. The RFL Academy was restricted to under-19s and BARLA assumed responsibility for under-18s and all younger groups. It seemed that peace had finally broken out. Soon afterwards the RFL and BARLA jointly launched Mini-League, which was a big success and there was a massive increase in amateur teams being invited to play in the Challenge Cup and Regal Trophy competitions.

The start of the 1993–94 season saw a further sign of rapprochement when the National Conference League was inaugurated as a joint venture between the two ruling bodies. To effect this the RFL was prepared to invest £250,000 over three years, but they stipulated that they wanted three clubs from the professional game to be included in the Premier Division. These were clubs that were essentially demoted from the professional game as underachievers, namely Blackpool Gladiators, Chorley Borough and Nottingham City, while Hemel Hempstead and eight amateur clubs – Askam, Dudley Hill, Egremont, Leigh Miners, Saddleworth Rangers, West Hull, Wigan St Patricks and Woolston – made up the rest of the Premier Division.

There were 32 teams in the three divisions. Woolston won the Premier Division title with Chorley Borough runners-up. Nottingham and Blackpool finished 11th and 12fth and it was not long before all three of the demoted professional clubs disappeared from the game. The RFL hoped that the National Conference League would enlarge the game's national profile. That was easier said than done, although the League was extended to 36 teams in 1994–95, including Northampton Knights.

The early 1990s saw significant changes in the rugby league landscape. David Oxley retired from the RFL in 1992 and it is hard to quantify just how big a loss to the game he was. Maurice Lindsay took over as chief executive and was as different from David as can be imagined in style and attitude. Oddly enough, we got on quite well, which will probably surprise some people. If I was previously one of the two Os, I was now one of the two Maurices – or three, if you count Maurice Bamford. In 1993 Rodney, later Sir Rodney, Walker took over as chairman of the RFL. He was another man who made life interesting as well as problematic for some of us in rugby league.

Sadly, in 1994, just after BARLA's 21st birthday, we lost two great men within a couple of days. Tom Keaveney died on 29 March, aged only 59, and on 1 April Jack Clayton passed away, aged 81. Their loss was a shattering blow to BARLA, especially as their deaths were so close together. They had been at the forefront of BARLA affairs from the very start, had been stalwart fighters and protectors of the Association. Tom was awarded the MBE while Jack had been presented with the Queen's Silver Jubilee medal in 1977 and both were awarded Life Membership of BARLA. Tom was succeeded by Nigel Hollingsworth as BARLA's national secretary.

I compile the Annual Report in the *BARLA Handbook* in 1994, which Tom usually did. I wrote: "Tom and Jack were the men who rescued amateur rugby league from the abyss back in the early 1970s. They had the courage and foresight to stand up and be counted. As national secretary and chairman respectively, they led from the front. During their time, they saw the Association grow from little more than 150 teams ... to something in excess of 1,350 teams today – such was their success. They will go down in rugby league history as all-time greats of the game and their monument, in BARLA, is there for all to see."

April 1995 put everything else deep in the shade in the world of rugby league. That is when Rupert Murdoch's Super League bombshell exploded, just when we were all ready to celebrate the game's centenary. What a year that was – £87 million into British rugby league coffers, massive loyalty payments for players who had never heard of Super League until someone offered them the money, summer rugby, another shake-up of the league format and rugby union went professional. It was almost impossible to make it up.

In the months after the announcement of Super League, I was rebuked by Graham Carden, the president of the New Zealand Rugby League, and then by Kath Hetherington, president of the RFL, for my links with the Australian Rugby League. I must admit my sympathies were with the ARL, and particularly with Ken Arthurson, their executive chairman. Ken Arthurson had been a firm supporter of BARLA for many years, appreciative of our contribution to spreading the game in the southern hemisphere and helpful to us in achieving that spread. However, BARLA really did not have a position on the whys and wherefores of the Super League War. We had enough problems of our own without interfering in matters that were the concern of the professional game.

However, I did feel it was my duty to ascertain if any of the Murdoch money was going to be directed to the grassroots of the sport. After all, BARLA had been bringing public money into the game for over 20 years by then, as well as providing countless players for the professional clubs. If there was even the possibility of five per cent of the Murdoch millions being invested into the amateur game, it would be an enormous boost for the development of grassroots rugby league, helping perhaps to attract more soccer and rugby union players to have a go at our game in the summer months.

Nothing ventured, nothing gained, so I wrote to Mr Murdoch. I asked if there was any provision for the amateur game in his new world order. It was quite a time before I got a reply. Essentially the answer was no, unless the RFL wanted to pass any monies on. It was entirely their business.

Unfortunately, the RFL's business also now seemed to involve undermining BARLA. This was a great shame. Only a couple of years earlier, matters had improved with the agreement over youth rugby and a move towards a unified game seemed possible – a game ruled by one body. The Sports Council wanted all sports to be governed by solitary bodies and that meant conjoining the amateur and professional elements of the sport. Crucially, it was decided that public monies would, at a time not too far in the future, be directed to the ruling body, which in essence meant the professionals, who would then disburse what accrued to the various parts of the sport. Previously, public monies were reserved for amateur sport. To some of us this new arrangement did not appear to be progressive or just and it would soon become a huge problem for BARLA.

Centenary year should have been a gigantic celebration of rugby league but the effect of the Murdoch deal actually put it in the shade and certainly complicated relations between various factions in the game. BARLA was excluded from the Emerging Nations Competition, which was part of the 1995 Centenary World Cup. Fair enough, some might say, because BARLA was obviously not a nation. But this was the centenary of rugby league, for heaven's sake, and BARLA had done more than its fair share in promoting the game in previously rugby league-free countries. As a sop, we were promised a game against the winners of the Emerging Nations, but even that failed to materialise and, ironically, Centenary year was one of the quietest in years for BARLA's international programme.

Another irony of this period was that moves toward unification had actually proceeded quite well under the auspices of the Sports Council. I attended a meeting at Chapeltown Road on 30 May 1995 along with Billy Gill, BARLA's chairman. We had productive talks with Rodney Walker and Maurice Lindsay. It was the first time the BARLA chief executive and chairman had ever sat down with their professional counterparts to discuss major policy since the appointment of Rodney Walker as chairman of the RFL and, it should be noted, Walker was also chairman of the Sports Council at that time.

Everything blew up again in January 1996 when BARLA suspended dialogue with the RFL after they moved to try to take over the National Conference League despite previous assurances that they had no intention of doing so. The RFL made a £300,000 offer to the National Conference League to defect from BARLA and went so far as to offer financial inducements to 100 top BARLA clubs to enter a competition run entirely by the RFL.

If that was not trying to dismantle BARLA, I don't know what it was. Our secretary, Nigel Hollingsworth wrote in his annual report in the *BARLA Handbook:* "During the year there were the usual disputes with the RFL which escalated to such an extent that financial inducements were offered to certain leagues to defect from BARLA. Fortunately, all our leagues, to their credit, held fast and resisted the overtures made –

let us hope there are no more backdoor attempts to dismember our Association." Some hope!

I was certainly getting some flak in this period. John Ledger of *The Yorkshire Post*, a journalist whom I have always admired, laid into me. On 1 February 1996 he wrote: "While the RFL's negotiating team has changed constantly over the last decade, the one constant factor in the unification equation has been Maurice Oldroyd, BARLA's longstanding chief executive. Oldroyd it was who failed to reach agreement with Jepson. Oldroyd it was who failed to reach agreement with Mitchell. Oldroyd it was who failed to reach agreement with Oxley. Oldroyd it was who failed to reach agreement with Lindsay. Oldroyd it was who failed to reach agreement with Walker. And Oldroyd it is who is now at loggerheads with [Kath] Hetherington." John went on to suggest that Maurice Oldroyd "may be the stumbling block to progress." Perhaps others agreed with him. In fact, I am sure some did.

However, I considered I merely had BARLA's best interests uppermost in my mind. BARLA was a democratic organisation. It was certainly not a dictatorship and I was just one of a six-man committee answerable to the membership of the Association, which meant its clubs, its leagues and its players. My job was to look out for BARLA's welfare and that did not involve throwing away its sovereignty. It was essential that BARLA retained its autonomy, even if the game adopted a unified structure. After all, some of us remembered the state of the amateur game when it operated under the control of the RFL.

There was even a suggestion "from one league member who claimed that [Oldroyd's] self-interest in protecting his salary and position was hindering the negotiating process." I would not have minded so much if it were not so preposterous. Only 18 months previously I had been offered a post by the International Board, covering the northern hemisphere, which carried a larger salary, a car – which I didn't have with BARLA – and the opportunity to travel the world. I love travelling! I turned it down to stay with BARLA.

BARLA did not follow the professional clubs and stuck to a winter season. We also hosted the Australian Aboriginals for the first time in the 1996-97 season, drawing the tests 1–1. Our youth squad toured Australia the following summer, but found the Australian Schoolboys too strong in the two tests, which ended in heavy defeats.

In May 1997, the Summer Conference League was launched. This was in our strategic plan. At BARLA, we thought it was a huge success. There were only 10 teams initially, they got going themselves and brought teams into the game. Bev Risman was one of the main people involved, and then Julian Harrison, who was subsequently employed by the RFL, became their first administrator.

We wanted to be involved with everyone playing rugby league. One important change was that rugby union grounds were now available to amateur rugby league teams more easily, because rugby union had started to allow professionalism in 1995.

Meanwhile, unification talks had been put on hold again, this time at the request of the RFL, who had formed a working party with a view to restructuring their internal organisation. Until that was done, they reckoned by May or June of 1997, any progress on unification would have to wait.

That wait appeared to be over at last when on 16 October 1997 the formation of a Joint Policy Board was announced. BARLA chairman Mike Morrissey and Sir Rodney Walker (RFL chairman) signed the relevant document. Five representatives from BARLA and five from the RFL were to form the Joint Policy Board under Sir Rodney Walker's chairmanship and meetings were to be held on a monthly basis. I thought the arrangement was a good one, one that had a chance of succeeding where all others had failed.

I was still getting plenty of criticism from various quarters, but I did not anticipate what happened in June 1998. I got the sack. No doubt some people probably thought it was about time, but it came as quite a shock. I was 62 and so not far from retirement. I was suspended from my duties on 4 June and on 23 July had my contract terminated with immediate effect. The architects of my dismissal were BARLA's chairman and vice-chairman, Mike Morrissey and Stuart Sheard. Both were absolutely first-rate amateur rugby league enthusiasts, who had done a great deal for the game and deservedly earned their positions as senior officers in BARLA. I understand that in sporting politics there are always rivalries. People think they can do a better job than the present incumbent. I was used to people undermining, criticising and denigrating senior officers. It goes with the territory, as they say.

Anyway, I ended up being kicked out of office. Enough people must have thought BARLA could have been run better, although I struggled to see what I had done wrong. Perhaps, I conceded, I had got behind on some office work, not written the right letters. Mike and Stuart clearly thought BARLA needed a change and that I was part of the problem and not the solution. Mary, of course, was livid – probably more so than me. So were a lot of other people. The charge against me was actually one of "undermining the authority of elected officers."

I was particularly well supported by Bob McDermott and Bob Scott, who were prominent members of FASDA (the First and Second Division Association – the professional clubs outside Super League), who had moved their headquarters into the BARLA offices. I was also inundated with support from members of BARLA, who wanted Mike and Stuart to be removed from office rather than me. The Sunday before my contract was terminated 22 of BARLA's 42 leagues attended a special meeting and passed a 19–0 vote of no confidence in Mike Morrissey and Stuart Sheard, who were relieved of their positions with immediate effect. I lodged a formal appeal against my dismissal and was reinstated. It was an episode I could have done without, of course, but such things often jolt one out of complacency or provoke heart trouble.

I had been particularly heartened by an open letter of support from Ken Arthurson. The full letter is produced as an appendix in this book, but the conclusion was "Mr Oldroyd is a man of the highest possible integrity and rugby league can afford to lose people of his calibre."

In November 1998 the Joint Policy Board negotiated a five-year agreement, at the end of which unification was scheduled to be achieved. As far as I was concerned, the creation of the Joint Policy Board was one of the best things to happen for years in the relationship between the amateurs and professionals and offered a genuine route to a unified structure. Moreover, I was a signatory.

The spat over my dismissal made me focus a bit more on my eventual retirement, which was due to happen in November 2000. When the dreaded day dawned, I had probably just about come to terms with the idea. Just two years earlier, BARLA's patron, Tom Mitchell, had died. Tom was one of my heroes and his death was a desperately big loss to rugby league and a sharp shock to me. A month before I retired, I had a heart operation and a pacemaker fitted. This caused Mary and I to abandon our plan to take a celebratory holiday at the Olympics in Australia.

My final couple of years as chief executive/special projects director at BARLA were in fact very gratifying. In December 1999, I was surprised to be given the Rugby League Merit Award by the Parliamentary All-Party Rugby League Group at their annual dinner at the House of Lords. Lord Lofthouse of Pontefract, chairman of the Group and BARLA's president for several years past, presented the award. Apparently, I was the first person from the amateur game to have the distinction. Lord Lofthouse also made a presentation to me on my 65th birthday, my official retirement, at the Wales versus Australia World Cup semi-final. That was a particularly pleasing and emotional experience because it happened in Huddersfield at the McAlpine Stadium.

Just as special for me, though, was BARLA's admittance to the 2000 Emerging Nations competition, which ran alongside the World Cup. The icing on my retirement cake came in the form of BARLA's defeats of Morocco and Japan in the group games and our 20–14 triumph over Italy in the final at Dewsbury.

It was not a bad way to sign off.

Presentation by Lord Geoff Lofthouse to mark Maurice's retirement

Maurice with Ron McGregor. They worked together on the
International Board for many years.

Spreading the word – with local kids on holiday.

Adam, Mary and Maurice enjoying a social occasion.

Maurice took Adam to Wembley to watch Adam's favourite
football team: Manchester City.

# 11.  Retirement – of sorts

So there I was – 19 November 2000, 65 years old, retired and on a pacemaker. I knew that I had to slow down a bit, but I also knew that I would never stop. Actually, there was never much chance that I would fade into the background. I have always been active, curious and wanting to do things and the passion that I have for all things rugby league and particularly the amateur game ensured that I would remain involved – probably until I pop my clogs.

Sadly, less than a year after my retirement, on 12 November 2001, Mary died. Mercifully, she died peacefully in her sleep next to me. Her death was so sudden and unexpected. She had not been ill. She was only 65, just six months younger than me. We had been married for 37 years – good years, happy years. Earlier that day we had attended Great Britain's 20–12 victory over Australia at the McAlpine Stadium and had had a wonderful time. Mary was probably just as familiar to rugby league folk as I was. She loved the game and contributed considerably toward it in terms of hard work and passion, as well as putting up with me.

With her gift for languages Mary was the official translator for the International Board, the RFL and BARLA on various trips to France and at home internationals. She was invariably presented with little gifts for her services and they are still scattered about the house, permanent memories of nice times. She was the PRO for Elland Amateur Rugby League Club for many years, wrote the match reports for the newspapers and served on all sorts of committees at the club and in the wider community.

There are a lot of excellent female administrators in BARLA. I have always thought that women are better organisers than men – they probably have a gene for organisation. It is pleasing that BARLA now have a woman, Sue Taylor, as chairperson.

Mary was a petite woman, but an amazingly good golfer. For a slender woman she could hit a golf ball a heck of a distance. We were both members at Elland Golf Club, but she was a better player than I was. She was also a good tennis player and won a lot of Bridge competitions down at Elland Golf Club, where she liked to play against the older members.

I know Mary was well respected in her profession – she spent her entire teaching career at Sowerby Bridge Grammar/High School and was a National Teachers' Award adjudicator. In the wider world she achieved a lot too, working hard for various local societies. She was a founder member and trustee of the Elland-Riorges Twinning Committee, organising school exchanges between the two towns and revelling in the opportunity to use her French. She was also a member of Elland Probus Club, the Elland Fast-track Committee and the Southgate Methodist Church Tuesday Group. In fact, when I think of all the things she was involved in, I'm surprised she had any time for me. It was no surprise that Mary's funeral at Southgate Methodist Church in the middle of Elland was packed to the rafters. The lives of a lot of people were touched for the better by Mary, particularly the young.

Our only child, Adam was the light of Mary's life. He was 33 when Mary died and she was always waiting for the day when he would settle down and provide us with grandchildren. Adam has always been a strong-willed so-and-so, but we both knew how much he loved and respected us. Mary would have been delighted at how Adam's life has subsequently panned out.

Barely two months after Mary's death, on New Year's Eve 2001, Adam played for Elland against Sharlston Rovers in the BARLA Yorkshire Cup Final at Headingley. Like me, Adam played at half-back but, as he was getting on a bit, he came on to the field as a substitute after about an hour. Nine minutes from time he dropped a crucial goal which stretched Elland's lead to 11–6 and then in injury time he sealed Elland's 17–6 victory with a super try. Mary would have been so proud. Adam told the *Yorkshire Post* reporter, "If my mother is watching from up there she will be absolutely thrilled. We came good in the end and I'm sure she will be smiling right now." I am sure she was beaming from ear to ear.

Adam was a talented boy and very sporting. Mary decided we should get him into Bradford Grammar School, although I was not too keen on the idea because I thought such schools were a bit snobbish. Anyway, Mary was right, especially when it came to educational matters. He thrived there. Of course, he had to play rugby union and Bradford Grammar had a crack team. It didn't matter what game he played, he was good at whatever he tried. Besides, he played league at under-16 for Elland.

## Family life:

Left: With Mary, Nancy and David on holiday in San Francisco.

Below: With Mary on holiday at NASA in Houston.

Mary interpreting at Villeneuve.

1989: Maurice and Mary's Silver Wedding at Ingwood: John, Kath, Maurice, Mary, Adam and Nancy.

Left: Adam playing for England Students against Wales in Cardiff, February 1990.

Below: Adam on a coaching course, learning from Ellery Hanley and Phil Larder.

113

Left: Adam and Maurice dressed up for a formal occasion.

Middle: A recent picture of Adam and Maurice.

Bottom: Adam with his son Joseph at the races.

Sport trumped academic pursuits for Adam, but he went to Carnegie College, which was part of Leeds Polytechnic and trained to become a PE teacher. Leeds Polytechnic were Rugby League Grand Slam winners in 1989–90 and one of Adam's team-mates was Stuart Lancaster, the current England rugby union coach. Adam was a good rugby footballer, a quick thinker and an excellent field and goal kicker. He was so good that he represented England Students against Wales on 18 February 1990. By a strange coincidence David Oxley's son Mark was in the Welsh side.

Apart from playing for Elland until well into his 40s, Adam got good coaching qualifications. In 1991 he did his Level 3 coaching course at Loughborough and there is a nice photograph in our hall of Adam, Ellery Hanley and Phil Larder in action during the course. I think Adam and Ellery got the highest grades on that particular course. So Ellery was in good company. Adam taught at Brooksbank School in Elland and twice coached his under–11s to the curtain-raiser at the Challenge Cup Final, once at Wembley and once at Cardiff. He now teaches at South Halifax High School, Exley, which is designated a sports academy and is just down the road from Siddal Amateur Rugby League Club. His wife, Helen also teaches there.

A couple of months before Mary died my official involvement with BARLA was unexpectedly renewed. At the end of May 2001 the BARLA chairman, Terry Parle, suddenly gave up the post without forewarning any BARLA officials. The first most people knew about it was from the rugby league papers a few days before the BARLA general meeting was due. Terry was also chair of the National Conference League and a highly regarded figure in the amateur game. The papers reported that Terry resigned in order to spend more time with his grandchildren.

So BARLA was unexpectedly without a chairman and there was briefly a constitutional vacuum. I was asked to stand for the post, but said 'no'. I thought a younger person should do the job. Apparently some younger people were approached, but none of them wanted the post. With only one day to go before nominations closed I was approached again and to help the Association I agreed to stand. On 2 September 2001 I was elected BARLA chairman. Billy Gill, the BARLA vice-chair, stood against me. The vote was 23–12 in my favour, and Billy, another Huddersfield man, continued as vice-chair.

Huddersfield sporting personalities: Olympic athlete Derek Ibbotson MBE, Maurice, Olympic swimmer Anita Lonsbrough MBE, England World Cup winning footballer Ray Wilson MBE.

Adam with Maurice who is receiving his Rugby League Merit award from Richard Lewis, Executive Chairman of the RFL at the John Smith stadium. (Photo: Varley Picture Agency)

There's some rugby league talent at this social event held by Tony Capstick. From left: Johnny Whitely, Billy Boston, Neil Fox, Peter Fox, Ian Brooke, Gary Hetherington, Roger Millward, Ray French, Maurice, Tony Capstick, Peter Harrison, Sam Morton, Brian Cole.

And their wives and partners: Back row: Molly Fox, Janice Brooke, Dai Harrison, Carol Millward, Janet Cole, Joan Fox; front: Karen Whitcombe, Helen French, Julie Capstick, Joan Boston, Tina Capstick.

117

Of course, there were some people who thought it was a case of Oldroyd being unwilling to let go, but I genuinely had no intention of becoming BARLA chairman at that point in my life. Two years later I was re-elected chairman and held the position until 2005.

Those four or so years were pretty traumatic. It was certainly no bed of roses being BARLA chairman. Unification with the RFL was sanctioned on 26 January, 2003 when BARLA voted 24–10 in favour of accepting the constitution of the RFL, just about 30 years after the schism between the two bodies. Despite unification there were still enduring problems – the perennial disputes about governance of youth rugby, the problem of the 12-month player, the financial hiatus caused by Sport England's redirection of grants to the RFL rather than straight to BARLA – the list seemed endless.

I came in for a lot of flak and was caricatured as reactionary, unable to accept a new world order and always ready to undermine anyone who did not share my views. Apparently, I was "on an ego trip". I was castigated in the press by John Ledger, Trevor Hunt and Terry Parle, to name just three, while the new executive chairman of the RFL Richard Lewis famously bashed BARLA as "not fit for purpose", quoting a Sport England audit. That seemed a bit rich to many rugby league people, coming from the RFL. What the RFL never seemed to appreciate was that BARLA was a democratic organisation. It was the sum of its players and clubs and the tens of thousands of volunteers who serviced them. You can't dictate to volunteers. They vote with their feet. By this time the Joint Policy Board had become history. Under that system decisions had been made by consensus and BARLA had equality in voting power with the RFL. Under unification the Community Board comprised 38 votes, of which BARLA only had three and crucially all public monies were directed to the RFL; small wonder that BARLA felt marginalised.

It is interesting to look at the *Rugby League Policy Board report 1997 – 2000*. Dr Hamish McInnes, on behalf of Sport England, wrote that "Established in late 1997 the Board has provided new leadership and vision, a co-ordinated plan for the development of the game, and a new spirit of co-operation between all arms of the sport... 'Progress through Partnership' aptly sums up a unity of purpose shared by both the RFL and BARLA." The conclusion of the report said that "The quite staggering achievements of the Rugby League Policy Board in little over three years represents a quantum leap in terms of the game's development. The National Development Strategy has woven its way into the fabric of rugby league culture and has highlighted just what can be achieved when all faces of the game work in a co-ordinated fashion for the greater good of the greatest game."

I was not against unification, but I did want a fair, equitable and democratic structure that safeguarded the Association's interests. As the years rolled on it appeared that certain elements in the RFL believed that BARLA was well past its sell-by date and would have been delighted to see it airbrushed from history. Ultimately, however, I believed that our existence would be safeguarded by the unification agreement, which stated "BARLA and the RFL shall remain as separate organisations and for the avoidance of doubt the RFL shall not have power either to amend the constitution of BARLA or to dissolve BARLA". This remains as important now as when it was first signed. I am no longer sure that even that safeguard will guarantee BARLA's future. I hope I am wrong.

In a sense unification was something akin to a shotgun wedding, forced on BARLA in January 2003 when Sport England performed a U-turn. They decided to change their policy from stopping all grants to both bodies if unification were not to be achieved, to suddenly stopping grants to BARLA alone. That took away all of BARLA's negotiating capacity. BARLA basically had no choice.

In June 2005 I stood down as BARLA chairman. I had probably done as much as I could and I was pushing 70 years of age, so, as the Bible says, I had had my three score years and 10. I was honoured to receive Life Membership of BARLA in 2005 and was amazed to be inducted on to the Rugby League Roll of Honour in the same year. Although the Roll of Honour contained such great players as Frank Myler, Johnny Whiteley and Bev Risman, I was particularly thrilled to be joining Harold Swift, a BARLA stalwart from the Blackbrook club in St Helens, who was also inducted in 2005. Harold was one of amateur rugby league's greatest servants, who had also been honoured with the MBE. I admired Harold as much as any other man I ever came across – a superb ambassador for our sport and a lovely family man.

After stepping down from the BARLA chair, and being succeeded by York's Spen Allison, I was offered the choice of becoming BARLA president or patron. After long consideration I accepted the position of patron. The main reason I chose to become patron of BARLA was to follow in the footsteps of the great Tom Mitchell. Tom had died back in 1998 and BARLA had not replaced him. I truly consider it a privilege and honour to be only BARLA's second patron. Just to be in the same bracket with Tom is something special. Of course, living in the BARLA heartlands I am able to be a more active patron than Tom was. Living in West Cumbria and heavily engaged in the professional game, not to mention his many other activities, Tom had less scope for hands-on involvement, but brought gravitas and influence to the position. Tom tended to gravitate to where the troubles of the world emerged.

I see the position of patron as essentially ambassadorial, involving meeting influential people in sport and promoting amateur rugby league. I hope that I come across as non-political and there is no monetary reward involved. Apart from being BARLA patron, I have been the Halifax ARL's representative to BARLA for quite a number of years, attending their meetings at Halifax Irish Club. I am a life member at Siddal ARL Club and am president of Yorkshire County. Another league I have always supported is the Yorkshire Junior League. I still have a good relationship with Colin Handforth, who has been involved with them for many years.

I still go to lots of matches. I tend to watch the professionals at Halifax and Huddersfield on Sundays, but I generally get to all the big games as well. Naturally I get to lots of amateur rugby league matches, often more than one match in an afternoon – I rarely see a game from start to finish as I like to get about and see the grassroots people who make our game tick.

One issue facing the game now is whether amateur teams should play a winter or summer season. I think that amateur players should all play in the winter, especially in the north. If the only summer rugby was the professional game, it would be better for the professional clubs' gates. Players and their families go and watch the professional clubs in the rugby league areas; they can't do that if they clash with the amateur matches. Family holidays are another problem with amateur summer rugby. BARLA now mainly works with the leagues that play in winter, such as the Pennine League. The identification of clubs as Community Amateur Sports Clubs is still very important, because they can then have charitable status, and access various grants and benefits.

Apart from the matches I go to countless rugby league functions, dinners and fund-raisers. I enjoy seeing old friends, such as Ray French, who was always very helpful to BARLA. He always gave us credit for what we were doing and would always help if we asked him.

I am a regular at the Houses of Parliament, where the All-Party Rugby League Group has its monthly meetings. I really enjoy my trips to London, even though the train journeys are quite tiring as I get older. Another monthly engagement is at the Huddersfield Senior Giants, which usually attracts interesting speakers. So, all in all, I am kept pretty busy in my retirement.

I still attend the monthly meetings at Westminster of the All-Party Parliamentary Rugby League Group. I remember working with David Hinchliffe, who was MP for Wakefield, and Sir Ian McCartney, who together set up the Group in 1987.

Another project I find very interesting is the Huddersfield RL Heritage Project, ably run by Brian Heywood. I attend their meetings when I can. The project brings back a lot of memories of my early Fartown days.

Apart from the rugby, I now have three lovely grandchildren – Sophia, Joseph and William. They all call me Maurice, by the way, not granddad. Adam and Helen made good use of me for the school run. Some people would call it exploitation. However, since I had a hip replacement in January 2013, I am less nifty on my feet and have to rely on taxis, so the school run looks unlikely to trouble me too much in the future.

Rugby league has been good to me. It has been my lifelong passion and I have been lucky enough to have earned my living in its service. It has provided me with entertainment, lasting friendships and the opportunity to travel. I have met royalty, politicians of all hues and celebrities of all types. I have had the privilege of meeting many of the greatest players that have graced our game and have had the good fortune to go on several trips to Australia and New Zealand with Peter Banner tours, which has enabled me to cement friendships with fabulous figures such as Billy Boston, Neil Fox and Alex Murphy, as well as to catch up with overseas administrators like Ken Arthurson, Ron McGregor and John MacDonald.

I was surprised, and delighted, to be given the Rugby League International Federation's 'Spirit of Rugby League Award' during the Rugby League World Cup in November 2013. It was in recognition of 'his commitment to international development over more than four decades' and was presented by Dean Carter, the RLIF chair.

Above all, fate pushed me in the direction of amateur rugby league and it took over my life. People sometimes ask me what it is about amateur rugby league that captivated me so thoroughly. Well, for a start it is a family game, which engages kids, parents and grandparents and brings communities together. It makes young players disciplined in a competitive environment. It teaches players to give and take knocks, which they will need to do in other aspects of their lives. It will provide them with a longer fuse when things go wrong and it will certainly provide friendship and camaraderie in large dollops.

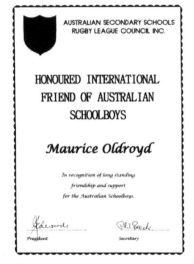

Finally, I would like to repeat the words I wrote in my final report as BARLA Chairman in 2005: "I extend a big thank you to all my friends on the International Board past and present. I also offer my sincere gratitude to the many people, professionals and amateurs alike, who have encouraged and supported me during my career at BARLA and in the wider world of sport."

# Appendix 1: Bill Fallowfield Circular re BARLA and Tom Keaveney's reply

"Correspondence has been addressed to this League and to the Sports Council purporting to come from an organisation which has adopted the title 'The British Amateur Rugby League Association'. It would appear that the persons who formed this organisation have no constitutional rights to do so.

The Rugby Football League will not recognise any unconstitutionally appointed body. Any club, league, official or player wishing to be affiliated to same will automatically sever connection with the Rugby League and will consequently lose any benefits derived from that connection e.g. assistance in ground rents, inter-town subsidies, compensation for players signed by senior clubs, proceeds from charity matches, grant aid or loans from the League, entry into League and County Cup Competitions, consideration for representative honours, etc.

The Sports Council will not recognise any organisation which is not in turn recognised by the sport's appropriate governing body. Whilst on the subject of the Sports Council, it would appear that there has been an attempt to mislead people into thinking that the present constitution of the League reduces the chances of amateur clubs receiving grant aid. This is simply not true.

As you know, moves are afoot to bring about changes in the Constitution whereby the game can benefit from other assistance the Sports Council may be able to offer in development and coaching schemes but I would like to make it quite clear that such assistance does not cover the week-to-week running expenses of clubs. So far there has been a poor response from amateur clubs to my circular RFL/42/73 dated 23rd January. The lack of replies could be taken to indicate that amateur clubs are satisfied with things as they are. If this is not so then do let me have your views.

In the meantime the League reminds all that any changes that may be made will be done constitutionally or not at all. Those District Leagues and clubs which have submitted claims for inter-town subsidies and ground rents will be paid, if such claims are approved, only on the understanding that they are in no way affiliated with any unconstitutional body".

**Tom Keaveney's reply:**
I have no doubt that the recent circular from Mr Fallowfield ... was read by you with great disappointment, our Association being representative of the amateur game, and by the almost unanimous support we have received we clearly are also disappointed, but it did not really come as any great surprise as Mr Fallowfield had stated in a recent press article that it was time he wielded the big stick at those moaning minnies within the amateur game, etc ... and such an irresponsible statement by a paid servant of the Rugby League can only lead to such a circular. Despite the fact that our Association has made it abundantly clear, on all occasions and to all people concerned, that it was our intention to, and STLL IS, to work with a close liaison with the Rugby League at Leeds, a circular of this kind is issued. There has been no reply direct from [the] Rugby League to our letter requesting a meeting to talk over matters. Instead we receive a rebuff like this in the form of a circular.

I would like to deal with this circular paragraph by paragraph, and the first is the point on being unconstitutional. The English (sic) constitution allows everyone the right of free association, so on what grounds does he base his argument that we are unconstitutional? People who have expressed an interest in the Association are quite free to do so, without breaking any constitutional rule of the Rugby League. [The RFL] appear to be attempting to deny the right of those in the amateur game to associate with each other for the benefit of the amateur game. To emphasise my point on this, I would draw your attention to the English Schools Rugby League who are totally autonomous, and this is all we ask.

123

With regards to the loss of benefits: a). Ground rents. The amounts that clubs receive will not, I'm sure, cause them to break up if they don't receive them. b). Inter-town subsidies. Again District Leagues will not suffer a great loss if they are not forthcoming. c). Compensation for players. It is thought that the amounts paid are far too low, and this is the opinion of practically the whole of the amateur rugby league. d). Charity matches. Surely this is a local issue and it is in the interest of the senior clubs to foster their local league as quite a number of their players come from it. e). Grants, etc. These will still apply with our Association. f). Entry into League cup and County cup. The Association would run their own competitions. g). Representation. Again the Association would attend to this.

One must ask the question, however, as to where does this money come from. Does it come from the British Playing Fields Association? If so, this is for amateurs and not professionals.

**Sports Council:** Mr Fallowfield is not the elected representative of the Sports Council, and he cannot speak for them. The Sports Council decide for themselves who they will recognise and who they will not recognise. Amateur sport is clearly set out in a Sports Council review of 1966/69, and it is interesting to note several facts and recommendations in this report. A). In all outdoor games there has been a remarkable growth in participation. B). Most governing bodies have submitted 4/5 year development plans [which] are already being implemented. C). A full-time secretary with supporting staff is essential together with full-time national coaches and development officers for the further development of a sport.

Last year the English Folk Dancers received £18,000 to cover administrative costs, and, as stated in earlier circulars, the Rugby Union has received £1 million in grants from the Sports Council. (Good luck to them). Last year almost 70 organisations took advantage of the tremendous assistance available and the number of national coaches has increased more than double, from 23 to 48.

The above points raise quite a few questions. 1). Why, with Chapeltown Road in charge, has our amateur game not achieved the same remarkable growth as all other outdoor sports? 2). Why, since Chapeltown Road were aware of the grants available from the Sports Council for the last seven years, has not the Rugby League taken advantage of them? When my own league applied for a grant of £33 for ground rent for the development of our Under 17 section, we were told that they would not tolerate late entries, and but for the help of our own senior club and supporters club we would not have been able to get under way. Yet the Rugby League can spend £15,000 on the administrative costs at Chapeltown Road to run the affairs of 30 clubs, and leave the amateur clubs in neglect, despite the Caine Report, [which] found this to be so.

Perhaps the answer lies in the Sports Council's own comment, 'Further development in the sport is intrinsically tied up with efficient headquarters administration'.

**Lack of replies from clubs:** Our answer to Mr Fallowfield's previous circular is the British Amateur Rugby League Association, who will govern all amateur rugby.

**Non-payment of ground rents, etc:** This, in my opinion, is the real rock bottom, that our so-called governing body can resort to tactics like this, for what it virtually amounts to is 'blackmail'. If we do not toe his line, then we have had it. I'm sure you must agree with me that statements like this must surely unite us all the more ... If we give in because of this, then we are, indeed, not worth our salt. Mr Fallowfield requires us to pay 50p affiliation fee each year and, as we do, we must be entitled to all benefits for that year. I am rather surprised that Mr Fallowfield has gone to the expense of sending circulars to all clubs and District Leagues, when one letter with one 3p stamp to me agreeing to a meeting may have set aside all their fears.

I deeply regret the length of this letter ... I wanted to cover all points to the full, and your Association is grateful for your continued support ... Rest assured that your Association, despite all obstacles, will endeavour to have a good working relationship with [the] RL. Surely, there must be someone at Chapeltown Road that appreciates what we are trying to achieve and will make some move to open negotiations."

## Appendix 2: Letter to Eldon Griffiths MP

"We as a Society firmly believe that 'any amateur sportsman should be free to play as many sports as he chooses at amateur level without fear or prejudice'.

Unfortunately, however, the Rugby Union (RU) do exercise blatant discrimination against the amateur rugby league player. We quote you paragraph 2.4, page 234 from the 1972–73 RU handbook which strengthens the regulations relating to amateurism: 'No person who is or has been associated in any active capacity with a non-amateur rugby club or organisation or an amateur club having any connection with a non-amateur rugby organisation, shall participate in the playing, refereeing, controlling, coaching, training, organising or administering of the game'.

The RU quite rightly and zealously guard their amateur status against the threat from the 30 non-amateur rugby league clubs, though one must hasten to add that there appears to be no such guard against professionals of any other sport, i.e. cricketers, playing rugby union, nor do the four Home Countries refuse games against France who actually play ex-professionals in their national sides. The RU by defending their own amateur status do, in fact, violate the very principles of amateurism, by denying the freedom of choice to other amateur sportsmen by discriminating against them. It is this principle we zealously defend, for this freedom of choice is part of our English heritage.

The situation is such, that should an enthusiastic rugby union player desire to try his hand at amateur rugby league, he must resort to subterfuge, for he knows that if his 'crime' is detected, his punishment is likely to be a 'life ban' from rugby union. We feel that such a restrictive practice is against the very principles of amateur sport, and particularly so when applied to youngsters in the 18-19 age group, for youngsters today often have an inclination to play several sports and any restriction on them can only be deplored in the strongest possible terms. For were a similar situation to apply to other sports, there would be, quite rightly, a hue and cry of national proportions by true sportsmen from far and wide.

Basing our argument on this sound and fair basic principle, with which we feel sure you as Minister of Sport will be in total agreement, the Rugby Union was asked, 'Can rugby players of any age change codes freely, provided that they are strictly amateurs who do not receive, directly or indirectly, payment or reward?' The RU reply was, 'the new regulations, which we quote above, eliminate any doubt of such a possibility which might have existed in previous regulations'.

For your information there are a mere 30 professional clubs who play the rugby league code, but what many people do not realise is that there are literally hundreds of amateur teams who play this fine sport for nothing more than 'the love of the game'. It is the rights of these players and not those of the professionals that we seek to protect. We are at a loss to understand how one amateur sport can so obviously discriminate against other amateur sportsmen, then blatantly incorporate such regulations in its official handbook for all to see. At the least, the above interpretation of the new regulations is discrimination in its worst form, immoral, unjust and against all the principles of English democracy and sportsmanship.

We should be obliged, therefore, if the above interpretations are correct, if you could kindly confirm whether such a situation will continue to exist whilst you are Minister of Sport.

We feel that with the Sports Council launching their campaign 'Sport for All" year in their efforts to encourage people to play more sports, the time is opportune to rescind this sporting anachronism and so have a more realistic attitude to sport in the seventies."

**M.F. Oldroyd**
**Press Officer, Huddersfield Rugby League Referees Society**
**October 1972**

# Appendix 3: Letters from Australia

**Letter of support from Ken Arthurson** (26 August 1998)

**To whom it may concern**

I am writing as the immediate past chairman of the Australian Rugby League and International Board, in reference to the recent dismissal of Mr Maurice Oldroyd from the position of chief executive officer of the British Amateur Rugby League Association.

The decision to take this action came as a considerable shock to me as I have always had the highest possible regard for Mr Oldroyd.

Based on my experience of more than 50 years in Rugby League as a player, coach and administrator, I have met few people possessing the dedication and passion for the sport of rugby league than Maurice Oldroyd. His unswerving loyalty and his determination for the success of that association, is reflected in the enormous increase in the number of teams in amateur Rugby League in Britain during his term of office.

During my term as chairman of the International Rugby League Board, I will say quite categorically that nobody contributed more to international development than Maurice. In fact, it is true to say that without the help of BARLA and tile guidance of Maurice Oldroyd the teams currently involved in rugby league from the south Pacific may never have got off the ground.

It concerns me that Mr Oldroyd's sacking may have been for reasons other than his ability to perform his duties. I say that because even as far back as four or five years ago I was aware that certain officials of the English Rugby League were scheming to get rid of Mr Oldroyd simply because he refused to accede to demands that he felt would be to the detriment of the amateur code in Great Britain.

I have taken the time to write on this matter because I sincerely believe that a great injustice has been done to this man. For his outstanding service to rugby league and the amateur code in particular, he really doesn't deserve this sort of treatment.

Mr Oldroyd is a man of the highest possible integrity and rugby league can ill afford to lose people of his calibre.

**K.R.ARTHURSON AM** (Chairman, Manly Warringah Rugby League Club Ltd)

**Letter from the Australian Secondary Schools RL Council** (10 March 2014)

Dear Maurice

I hope that you are well and enjoying good health. It is my honour to write to you and advise you that have been recognised as an *Honoured International Friend of Australian Schoolboys Rugby League.* At our recent Council meeting you were endorsed unanimously as a worthy recipient of this award for your longstanding friendship and support of the Australian Schoolboys whilst on tour to your shores.

Your work as BARLA chairman in ensuring that our two countries could compete on the field of play and enjoy the camaraderie off it can never be underestimated. It is through your leadership that players from both countries were exposed to international competition and provided experiences that would benefit them for the rest of their lives. It was always an honour and privilege to be in your company whenever we toured England. The current and past executives of the Australian Schoolboys value your friendship and regard this as a thoroughly deserved accolade. You along with the other inductees (Alf Sim, Jackie Reed, Andy Harland and Pascal Zanin from France) are the inaugural inductees for award of *Honoured International Friends of Australian Schoolboys Rugby League.* I plan to tour with the Australian side at end of 2014 and it would be my honour to personally congratulate and acknowledge you as one of the first worthy recipients of this award. In the meantime I have included a copy of *In a Class of their Own* (written to celebrate our 40th anniversary) and a shirt as a small thank you for the work that you have done for the Australian Schoolboys.

**Phil Beecher (ASSRL Secretary)**

# Appendix 4: The text from the booklet for The Official Opening of the British Amateur Rugby League Association Headquarters 30th Nov 1990.

In 1973, with £25 in the bank to fund what was a dream, the early BARLA pioneers could never have imagined that in just 17 years her Majesty the Queen would be opening their prestigious Headquarters. As current BARLA president, I can think of no greater accolade for our organisation. We really do seem to have come such a long way in such a short time.

Huddersfield has held the key to so many 'firsts' in our game from its birth in 1895 and it is fitting that we are sharing our day with the town. The Mayoral greeting will be given by our own National Development Officer, Tom O'Donovan and his pride I know will be ours. Huddersfield is a fitting home for BARLA and the generosity of the old West Yorkshire Authority ensured that our future is here.

However, the British Amateur Rugby League Association is more than a building. It is people scattered all over the country whose first love is rugby league. People who give of their time to train, coach, or organise, fund and develop our game. As amateurs we are proud of our traditions, our time is freely given to ensure that all who wish to participate can do so. From those with talent to play for their country, to those who take to the park for recreation, from the young to the not so young, there is a home for them all in BARLA.

Along with the Rugby Football League, our professional counterparts, we seek to establish a national identity. This will not be an easy task, but today's recognition is a big step forward. Our credibility is now well established.

With our game's Centenary so near, we have laid our plans for the future and the facilities we possess will help us realise those plans. In co-operation with the Sports Council, local authorities, the Rugby League Foundation and our sponsors, who together provide so much financial support, we from the highest to the lowest in our game, must draw strength from today and prove that rugby league is the greatest game in the world.

**David Knight**
**BARLA President**

### The BARLA Story

The game of rugby league football was founded at a meeting in the George Hotel in Huddersfield in 1895 – only yards away from the fine Victorian building which now houses the new Headquarters of BARLA – the British Amateur Rugby League.

BARLA itself is a "breakaway from a breakaway" having been formed — also in Huddersfield – in 1973 by a small band of amateur rugby league enthusiasts to "put the amateur game on a proper footing".

The 1895 break had to come when the Rugby Union steadfastly turned its back on all forms of professionalism – even refusing to allow amateur players to be recompensed for wages lost while they followed their sport. The 22 Northern RU clubs broke away to become the Rugby Football League.

BARLA began with a membership of 155 teams – and a £25 bank balance. Its growth, in less than 20 years, has been described as one of Britain's greatest sporting success stories with BARLA teams undertaking international tours, the establishment of thriving national league and cup competitions and coaching and training projects encouraging youth and schoolboy teams in almost every corner of Great Britain.

There are now around 1,100 teams registered with BARLA and on an average weekend in the season close on 50,000 players – amateurs and schoolboys will be in action. In 1990, the Association's National Cup attracted 221 teams, a world record for a rugby football competition under either code.

Amateur rugby league football is now played by 16 nations (compared to five when the Association was founded) and BARLA has been instrumental in arranging 17 international exchanges between Britain and rugby leaguers in Australia, New Zealand and the South Pacific – the 1990 tour including the Cook Islands, Western Samoa and Tonga.

The amateur game has also successfully spanned social and geographical boundaries in the UK. While retaining its roots in the industrial and coal mining areas of Yorkshire, Lancashire, the North East and Cumbria, it has spread to embrace Oxford and Cambridge Universities, the Armed Forces and teams in the Southern Counties, London, the Midlands and South Wales. In 1989, when England staged the Student World Cup, the first student teams from Ireland and Scotland took part.

BARLA has a declared aim of making amateur rugby league a truly national sport by 1995 – the centenary year of the 13-man code. The Sports Council has promised £640,000 between now and Centenary year which will be concentrated on fostering youth rugby and further expansion of the game beyond the old, traditional areas. The National League of 24 top sides has recently clinched a three-year £100,000 sponsorship deal with British Coal Opencast to aid development nationwide while Sports Council and local authority backing supported by the Rugby League Foundation, has enabled the appointment of 14 full-time development officers in many parts of the country.

One of the Association's proudest achievements has been to win the 'free gangway' between league and union so that a rugby union player can now take part in amateur rugby league games without fear of punishment – which has been as harsh as a lifetime ban. Prompted by the Sports Council, agreement was concluded in 1987 between the presidents, Bob Beal OBE of BARLA and Brigadier Dennis Shuttleworth of the RFU, the culmination of 15 years of patient negotiation and diplomacy. BARLA continues to play a major role in improving relationships in all areas of rugby football, and sport as a whole.

Amateurs learning and playing the game for the joy of it continue to be the mainstay of rugby football both at home and abroad, while the amateur game is justly proud of its contribution in players and playing skills to the top echelons of professional football.

Tough and fast in the field, rugby league retains an enviable record for sportsmanship and for spectator enjoyment and good behaviour. Throughout the massive expansion of the past 17 years the game has managed to maintain its reputation as a sport enjoyed by all the family and a sport which has kept its roots in the communities from which it sprang.

### Personality profiles

Tom Mitchell, as a member of the Rugby League Council, played a pioneering role in "setting free" the amateur code in 1973 – being the lone voice in the early days when the League voted 29–1 against the move to recognise BARLA. The Association acknowledged his contribution by making him its sole Patron.

Bob Beal OBE of Leeds, a past chairman of BARLA, and the Association's first president. He is now a life member and chief trustee.

Jack Clayton of Huddersfield, a founder member of BARLA and its first chairman – now a vice president and life member of the Association.

### Historical highlights

1973: The British Amateur Rugby League Association (BARLA) formed in Huddersfield with Jack Clayton as chairman, Tom Keaveney as secretary and Maurice Oldroyd as assistant secretary.

1976: Maurice Oldroyd appointed first full-time national administrator.

1977: First amateur rugby league tour to the southern hemisphere.   BARLA under-18s visit Australia and New Zealand in the Queen's Silver Jubilee year.

Amateurs, Cawoods, defeat professionals, Halifax in first round of the John Player Cup.

1978: Secretary, Tom Keaveney receives the MBE for services to amateur rugby league.

First BARLA open-age overseas tour - Papua New Guinea, Australia and New Zealand.

Oxford University ARL Club formed.

1979: BARLA hosts first England tour by Papua New Guinea.

First England visit by Australian Club, Tweed Heads Seagulls

Leigh invited to play French Champions, Catalan, in Perpignan.

1980: Australian Combined High School play historic test match against BARLA Youth at Headingley, Leeds.

First 'Varsity match' – Oxford defeat Cambridge.

North West Counties team, Shevington Sharks become first team to play in United States.

1982: Phil Larder appointed first full-time director of coaching.

BARLA open-age second tour to South Pacific.

Census confirms increase of 700 teams and 18,000 players in BARLA's first 10 years.

1983: BARLA youth team, the Young Lions, highly successful tour to New Zealand and BARLA hosts Maoris' first tour of Britain.

1984: BARLA president Bob Beal receives OBE for services to amateur rugby league.

First tour to Australia by Upper School and Colleges representative team.

1985: Leeds City Council, in conjunction with BARLA, appoint Maurice Bamford as first full-time development officer.

1986: West Yorkshire Metropolitan Council grant £150,000 to help acquire new headquarters.

Greater Manchester Council grant £180,000 to develop the game's first centre of excellence at Leigh.

Census shows 20,000 players and 800 teams.

Amateur Clubs return to the Rugby League Challenge Cup after five years' absence.

TV Documentary *Banned for Life* on relations between BARLA and the Rugby Union.

Great Britain open-age team tour of Australia – winning five games out of seven.

British Students ARL team compete in the inaugural Student World Cup held in New Zealand.

Australian Schoolboys, Junior Kangaroos, 100 percent success record in English tour.

National amateur rugby league successfully launched bringing the top 10 amateur clubs into one competitive National League.

Humberside amateurs, Myson's, beat the professionals of Batley in the John Player Special Trophy – only the second amateur club since 1909 to knock out a professional team in a major Rugby League competition.

1987: 176 teams enter BARLA National Cup- a world record for either code.

Introduction of the 'free gangway' allows the genuine amateur rugby player to play both codes ending almost a century of hostility between the two sports.

Formation of the Rugby League Foundation, a charity trust drawn from all sections of the game to encourage development particularly in youth, student and schoolboy rugby.

Papua New Guinea Tour England and play Great Britain at both professional and amateur levels.

New Zealand junior Kiwis 100 percent successful in English tour.

The Rugby League Joint Development Scheme formulated under the guidance of local authorities and other agencies for the benefit of Rugby League.

1988: Appointment of Tom O'Donovan as national development officer.

186 teams enter BARLA National Cup. Introduction of mandatory insurance for member clubs to cover for serious accident and public liability.

Appointment of Ian Cooper as administrative officer.

Director of coaching Phil Larder publishes the Rugby League Coaching Manual.

Opening of £250,000 Centre of Excellence at Leigh.

Formation at Westminster of a Parliamentary Rugby League All Party Group of MPs.

1989: BARLA moves into its new £250,000 headquarters building in a conservation area in the centre of Huddersfield – 'a short punt' away from the George Hotel where the game was born in 1895.

Four Nation Easter Tournament in the Netherlands comprising of eight teams from England, France, Germany and Holland.

Great Britain Young Lions (under-19) tour Australia.

The Second Student World Cup at York attracts a record eight nations – Australia, England, France, Holland, Ireland, New Zealand, Scotland and Wales.

Formation of Women's Amateur Rugby League Association.

National League expands to two divisions increasing membership from 10 to 22 teams.

Womens ARL send a Great Britain XIII to France for a two-match tour against regional teams.

1990: Record entry of 221 teams for the National Cup.

Sports Council grant aids the 1990 to 1994 forward plan to the sum of £640,000.

BARLA Lions historic tour to the South Pacific playing first ever internationals against the Cook Islands, Tonga and Western Samoa.

Record £100,000 sponsorship for the National League by British Coal Opencast.

Launch of the new BARLA Logo.

Formation at Strasbourg of a European Parliament Rugby League Inter-Group of MEPs.

First satellite television sportscast of an Opencast National League game - Wigan St Patricks versus Millom.

Official opening by Her Majesty the Queen of the new BARLA headquarters in Huddersfield.

### The National Development Scheme

The National Development Scheme was established in 1988 with the appointment by BARLA and the Rugby Football League of Tom O'Donovan as National Development Officer.

Main aim of the Scheme is to see rugby league played at all levels throughout the country. To this end there are already 14 full time Regional Development Officer posts established – thanks to the financial support of many local authorities, the Sports Council, the Rugby League Foundation the sponsors. Awareness and interest in the game has never been higher and expansion continues nationally with more schools and amateur clubs playing *every* season. Public awareness has been heightened at national *level* in recent times by such well publicised events as the tremendous final test victory against Australia in 1988 followed by a winning test series against New Zealand in 1990 and the headline-grabbing 1990 test performances against the Australian tourists – while the domestic season provides action-packed games to thrill thousands of spectators. The game is now well established outside the traditional playing areas. There are thriving amateur leagues in London, The Midlands, South West and Wales while further north the East Midlands League and the North-East league continue to flourish.

Significantly, clubs have recently been formed in Crewe, Wrexham, North Wales, Newmarket, Gateshead and Nene Valley – continuing the vital task of filling in gaps on the national map. These new clubs will provide important focal points for future development initiatives and act as catalysts for the formation of still more amateur rugby league clubs throughout Britain. Priority for a successful development programme must go to the introduction of the game into schools and colleges encouraging the formation of more junior and youth teams and women, as players, will continue to be a target group for recruitment. The Development Scheme also has the declared aim of having rugby league recognised and played by the uniformed services – in particular the Police and the Armed Forces. There are, therefore, potential target groups in almost all sections of the community. The requirements of a successful development programme aimed at spreading the game are enormous. We need more players – but we also need to recruit coaches, referees and administrators.

### The National Coaching Scheme

The National Coaching Scheme was reorganised in 1982 with appointment of Phil Larder, the first full-time director of coaching whose major priority was to improve the coaching and playing standards of the game. The visit of the 1982 Australian Kangaroos emphasised that British Rugby League was at an all-time low. The Kangaroos were undefeated on their 15 match tour, amassing 423 points and conceding only 80.

Larder closely studied the methods of Australian coach Frank Stanton and concluded that a coaching revolution was needed if Britain were ever to compete against Australia again. Trips to study the Australian Rugby League Coaching Scheme, a visit to the Los Angeles Rams in America and a further stay in Australia with Jack Gibson and Ron Massey helped to crystallise thoughts.

A plan of action was formulated to attack coaching at every level, from the important grass roots which are the lifeblood of any sport, through to the international team at the pinnacle. With the help of the National Coaching Foundation, the Coach Accreditation courses were completely reorganised into three distinct and progressive levels. These are now widely acclaimed by other governing bodies of sport, supported by the Sports Council and encouraged by education authorities and institutes of higher education throughout the country.

In 1985 the Rugby Football League insisted that all those coaching professional players must hold a Level 2 Grade 1 Certificate and BARLA followed suit by encouraging all coaches involved with the game at any level to progress through the Scheme, and selecting as representative coaches only those who held a Level 2 Grade 1 Certificate or above. As more coaches progressed through the three levels, improvement became more apparent each year. The game in the 1990s has never been healthier – it is exciting and stimulating to play and entertaining to watch.

The purpose-built BARLA Centre of Excellence on a 7-acre site at Leigh has become a focal point for specialist coaching at all levels. At any one time international and county squads from school, student, youth and open-age teams might be seen in action on the three floodlit pitches. The excellent indoor and outdoor facilities also attract Civil Service and Womens representative sides as well as the Great Britain professional team.

As with other sports the standards of the game are judged by the performance of the international team. Equally important, the coaching philosophies at this level are taken back to clubs by the International players. Phil Larder, therefore, has been actively involved with the International team since 1985, first working as Maurice Bamford's adviser and more recently with Malcolm Reilly. The tremendous gaps which existed between Great Britain and both New Zealand and Australia have been gradually and systematically closed. Examine the facts:

1. 9th July 1988. Third test. Sydney. Australia 12 Great Britain 26. Although the test series was lost, this was the first victory on Australian soil for 14 years.
2. 11th November 1989.      Third Test. Wigan. Great Britain 10 New Zealand 6. The first test series win against New Zealand for 24 years.
3. 24th June 1990. Second Test. Auckland. New Zealand 10 Great Britain 11. The first test series win in New Zealand for 11 years.
4. 27th October 1990. First Test. Wembley. Great Britain 19 Australia 12 The first victory against Australia on home soil for 12 years.

In the last eight years rugby league in Britain has come a long way, further, perhaps, than any other sport.  The National Coaching Scheme is proud of the leading part it has played in this success story.


**Personality profiles**

Hat-trick specialist Steve Critcheson of Ace Amateurs Hull is BARLA's most capped player and has been Player of the Year twice and Great Britain captain.

The only man to win BARLA's Player of the Year award on three occasions, Dave O'Connor of Yew Tree, Leeds – seriously injured when playing for Great Britain against France in 1987.

Mick Keebles of Dudley Hill ARLFC (Bradford) – BARLA's 1989–90 Player of the Year. He came to prominence in the student game, captaining England's Student side in the World Cup and now plays professional rugby with Halifax.

131

## Appendix 5: Obituary: Mary Oldroyd by Robert Gate

Mary Oldroyd was living proof that rugby league's soul and heartbeat does not dwell anywhere near Red Hall or Sovereign House. She was of much more fundamental use and value to the game than any amount of chief executives, football managers and directors with big titles. I had known Mary only a few years and wish it had been many more. The last time I saw her was on 3 November 2001. It was a miserable, murky Saturday afternoon and we were at the precipitous Goldfields ground at Greetland, where Elland were taking on Norland in the last 16 of the Yorkshire Cup.

Persistent drizzle into my spectacles forced me to abandon the bottom touchline and decamp for the higher ground, where the Norland team's entourage had taken up residence. Suddenly, I heard a woman's voice and immediately knew it was Mary's. She was not talking to me and was a long way off. She was wearing wellies, was well wrapped up, had her Cagoule hood over a woolly hat and was also protected by a huge red and yellow umbrella covered with *Rugby Leaguer* logos. She was a woman who knew what she was doing.

Throughout the match she patrolled the touchline. Everyone seemed to know her. She stopped to talk to locals and appeared to know a fair number of the visiting Humbersiders. All the while she was compiling the match facts for the reports which would go into the local papers. She had time for everyone. As the play ebbed and flowed she accompanied it up and down the touchline, passing the time of day with me as she and the Norland subs and officials trekked backwards and forwards.

At one point, probably at half-time, we had a chat about the current state of affairs in the game. This was about the time when there was much speculation in the press about the game going 'open' and in essence doing away with the concept of amateurism. Mary was furious at the idea. The day they began to pay players at Elland, she told me, was the day she would be out of there It was the sort of passionate vitriol to which the movers and shakers of the game should have been forced to listen. She spoke rugby league realpolitik and it would be as well if more high-powered administrators listened to people like Mary to give them a grasp of what grassroots rugby league really represents.

Before games, Mary and her sister Nancy Wilkinson, wife of David, the Elland secretary, usually had the task of collecting subs from the Elland players and after the games they were busy preparing the refreshments, along with other hard-working club members. As PRO for the club Mary, and Nancy, provided *The Halifax Courier, The Huddersfield Examiner, The Rugby Leaguer* and Andrew Bennett of the Pennine League with match details and reports. As a long-serving member of a female dominated committee, Mary also performed countless other tasks for the club's benefit and all for the usual reward of those involved at this level – nothing in financial terms, but heaps in human terms.

To say Mary was immersed in rugby league would be something of an understatement. A Siddal girl, daughter of a local farmer and a supporter of Halifax, she had to cope with being married to Maurice Oldroyd, a Fartowner at heart, and arguably the sole leading rugby league administrator to have emerged with honour and an enhanced reputation from the past decade of blood-letting. Her son, Adam, is an England student international half-back and scored the match-clinching try in Elland's victory over Sharlston in the Yorkshire Cup Final at Headingley on New Year's Eve, an occasion which would have delighted Mary.

Professionally, Mary – a first class honours graduate in French – spent her career teaching at Sowerby Bridge Grammar School. Her facility for languages equipped her well when she was called upon to act as translator/interpreter for the Rugby League International Board, the Rugby Football League and BARLA. Apart from rugby league, Mary was involved in numerous other local, civic and charitable organisations. She was a woman of immense energy, charm, fun and benign intent, who will be missed by all who had the good luck to have had their lives touched by her.